PYTHON
PROGRAMMING

publication of the trademark is without permission or backing by the trademark owner. All trademarks and brands within this book are for clarifying purposes only and are owned by the owners themselves, not affiliated with this document.

Table of Contents

INTRODUCTION

The python programming language is a current language for web programming originally designed and developed by Guido van Rossum in the 1980s. After this moment, Python has become an extensible and versatile programming language with high efficiency. Python is used by many of the world's largest platforms, such as YouTube, Reddit, as well as Disqus. Python has a variety of characteristics that make it an elegant language of programming. Such qualities comprise wedge-like reliability, object-oriented architecture, portability, and even a versatile standard library that contains a range of 3rd-party or even bundle packages.

Since the early 1980s, Python was under efficient development and therefore is considered to be an intelligent programming language. The Python language designers conducted significant productivity as well as regression evaluations to make sure that with each upgrade the language stay stable and error-free.

Python programming provides a range of qualities that make it an attractive option for the creation of web applications. Python programs are easily portable since for these current operating systems and certain embedded software tools, python interpreters are everywhere.

Python's object-oriented nature present it a perfect first preference for new programmers and easy to use from several other object-oriented languages to programmers switching to Python. Python programming is straightforward and supports a very strong software architecture and focus on object-oriented approach.

The standard Python library offers programmers with a range of attributes relative to languages that are much more complex, such as C, yet retaining the language syntax straightforward and easy. Comprehensive file-based I / O, server interactiveness, advanced error handling and a host of standardized details are aimed at making Python ideal for every system and also for diverse-based programming use. This makes python programming a seamless task for software designers looking for a path to the creation of web applications.

Python is known as a structured language with standard library and advanced features. However, the growing adoption of python programming has led to significant range of components or third-party packages that broaden the features of Python and thereby enable the language to deal with particular programming difficulties. For example, for managing non-standard repository communication and competent features of cryptography, modules are available. There are also modules for dealing with regular tasks, like testing metadata files, generating graphs, and assembling Python uses to structured runtime purposes. Python's web coding is much simpler because of the availability of numerous internet-centric components that can manage tasks such as email, retaining HTTP status, playing with JavaScript, and other common web creation tasks.

PYTHON PROGRAMMING

Python is object-oriented high-level programming language, an interpreter with a versatile syntax. Python is straightforward and easy. Its high-level structured data systems, combined with dynamic linking and adaptive typing, allow Advanced Application Development notably attractive. It's also used to connect pre-existing components together as scripting or perhaps as a glue language. It stresses readability and therefore reduces the cost of maintaining the software. Python promotes packages and plugins that facilitate the modularity of the program and also reusability of code. The Python compiler and the extensive standard library are rendered in source or perhaps binary form, absolutely freely distributed and free for all the major platforms.

Because of the higher efficiency python provides, many programmers love it. As there's no compiling phase at all, the process of edit-test-debug may be very quick. It's quick to fix Python programs: incorrect data or a mistake will never lead to segmentation error. Instead, it creates an exception as soon as the translator figures an error. If the program fails to recognize the exception, a stack trace is generated by the compiler. A supply number debugger checks global and local parameters, analyzes random statements, sets breakpoints, and moves a line in time etc. Within Python itself, the debugger is built, reinforcing the subjective nature of Python. Normally the fastest way to debug a program, on the contrary, is to apply a few print statements to the source: the rapid loop of edit-test-debug generally makes this simple process incredibly efficient.

THE EVOLUTION OF PYTHON LANGUAGE OVER THE YEARS

Python is among popular languages of coding. Python is also object-oriented as well as open source moreover it's a general-purpose and high-level programming language. Similarly, Python was used by a large number of developers around the globe to create GUI applications, smartphone apps and websites. The distinguishing aspect that Python has shown so far is the reality that by writing easy to read and concise code, it enables programmers to bring out more ideas. Furthermore, the developers may get advantage from various Python libraries to reduce the amount of time and effort required to develop large and complicated software applications.

A number of high-traffic sites such as Facebook, Web Therapy, Shopzilla, Linux Weekly News, Yahoo Maps including Yahoo Groups are now using the programming language. In contrast, Python is also used to develop software for learning, research, banking, and gaming. However, programmers tend to use different programming language variations Depending on Python's user information and also market share details, that was posted on W3techs, 99.4 per cent of websites are actually using Python 2 whereas only 0.6 percent of sites are using Python 3. That's precisely why this has become essential for every programmer to know and evolve the different versions of Python.

How exactly has Python been evolving throughout the years?

Conceived as a pastime Programming Project

While the extremely famous programming language of 2015, in December 1989, Guido van Rossum originally designed Python as a pastime project. As the office of Van Rossum stayed closed throughout Christmas, he was looking for a leisure activity that could keep him occupied throughout the holidays. He wanted to build an interpreter for a completely new language of scripting, and also called the Python project. In a result, then, Python was developed as a successor to the programming of ABC. Van Rossum turned the script available in February 1991 shortly after writing the interpreter. However, the Python Software Foundation is currently managing the open-source programming language.

Version one of Python

In January 1994, Python 1.0 was introduced. The primary launch had a mix of new functionalities, such as reduction, map, filter, and lambda, as well as functional programming tools. Version 1.4 has been released with several new functionalities like keyword arguments, built-in assistance for complicated numbers, and an easy way of encapsulating information. Two smaller updates, variation 1.5 in December 1997 and variation 1.6 in September 2000 preceded the primary launch. Python's version one missed the functionality of the famous programming languages, although the original ones established a good base for a revolutionary and efficient programming language to evolve.

Version two of Python

In October 2000, with a garbage management system, Python 2.0 was released with a refurbished display comprehension feature. Several other functional programming languages such as Haskell inspired the syntax for the show comprehension feature. However, unlike Haskell, Python 2.0 preferred alphabetic keywords over characters with punctuation. In addition, processing of comparison cycles was carried out by the trash collection unit. A couple of small updates preceded the primary release. Such updates included a range of programming language characteristics as support for nesting scopes, plus integration into an independent structure of the forms of Python and the class's right. The Python Software Foundation also confirmed that Python

2.8 would not exist at all. Nonetheless, version 2.7 of the programming language will be endorsed by the Foundation by 2020.

Version three of Python

In December 2008, Python 3.0 was released. It included several completely new innovations and improvements as well as a range of discontinued features. The discontinued functionality & reverse incompatibility made Python's 3rd version completely different from previous versions. Most programmers have opted to use Python 2.6 or maybe 2.7 to take advantage of the obsolete functionality of the last main version. Nonetheless, it was rendered more futuristic and famous by the completely new features of Python three. In reality, most programmers have switched to template 3.0 of the programming language to use such incredible features.

Python 3.0 substituted the print declaration with the built-in print() functionality, enabling programmers to use customized separator among rows. It also streamlined the comparison ordering instructions. In the event that the operands are not ordered in a logical and normal sequence, a Type Error condition may now be enhanced by purchasing comparison operators. Therefore, version 3 of the programming language uses information and text instead of 8-bit strings and Unicode. By definition, the management of each code as Unicode represents binary data as Unicode encrypted.

Programmers cannot access features like string exceptions, sessions of old model as Python three is backwards-incompatible, And the implicit imports of family members. In addition, the designers must be familiar with changes to the syntax and APIs. We can use anything called "2to3" to switch application quickly from two to three in Python By alerts and suggestions, the tool emphasizes regions of incompatibility and consideration. The comments help developers make changes to the code and adapt their existing implementations to the programming language's latest version as well.

Current Versions of Python

Currently developers can choose between version 3.4.3 or version 2.7.10. Python 2.7 enable developers to benefit from improved numeric management and standard library improvements. Furthermore, this version facilitates the migration of developers to Python 3. On the contrary, Python 3.4 features a number of new libraries and software modules, improvements to security and also updates to CPython implementation. Nonetheless, both in the Python API and the programming language, a set of functions are deprecated. Python 3.4 can tend to be used by designers to get help in the longer run.

Version four of Python

After the launch of Python 3.9, Python 4.0 is scheduled to be on sale in 2023. This will launch several improvements that help developers switch smoothly from version 3 to version 4. In fact, as they accumulate experience, skilled Python programmers may make use of a range of viable backward alternatives to restructure their existing applications with no extra time and effort. Nonetheless, to get a good description of Python 4.0, the developers still have to wait long. However, they will track the latest releases so that they can easily upgrade to the programming language version 4.0.

Python's versions two and three are entirely change from one another. That coder must, therefore, consider the roles of these particular versions and analyze their functions depending on some of the task's specifications. In particular, each programmer has to test out the Python edition that supports that application.

Nonetheless, each programmer must use the latest version of Python to maximize use of the new functionality and also provide long-term assistance.

PROS AND CONS OF PYTHON PROGRAMMING LANGUAGE

We want to be detailed about what we can do with it whenever we want to pick a new word for a job. They need to consider how it can encourage us to be successful about what we need to do, even if we want to be careful about the issues arising. So, we think it's worth stating these advantages and disadvantages.

Benefits of Python Programming Language

a. Extensive Libraries

Python comes with a vast library, as we found out in our post on Python's features. It includes coding for various purposes, like regular phrases, editing of images, email, CGI, databases threading, web browsers, system checking, creation of documents, and much more. You don't even have to write all of the coding on your own

B. Extensible

Python is familiar with many other languages, as we saw before. You can compose a code in languages such as C or C+, This is useful, especially when dealing with projects.

C. Embeddable

Python is also embeddable in contrast to extensibility. You can put the Python script in a different language's source code, like C. In the contrary language, it helps one to add scripting functionality to the code.

d. Improved Productivity

The versatility of the language and extensive libraries make programmers much more efficient than C and Java. In addition, you write less and achieve a lot more.

e. IOT Opportunities

Since Python is the basis of new platforms like Raspberry Pi, it is discovering a bright future for the Internet of Things. This implies connecting the word to real life.

f. Simple and Easy

You may have to produce a course to print' Hello World' when interacting with Java. However, in Python, this will only be done by a print statement. In comparison, finding, learning, and coding is very easy. This is exactly why, when people pick up Python, they have a hard time adjusting to several other languages like Java, which are wordier.

G. Readable

Using Python is just like using English words because it's not like a verbous script. This is also the explanation of why finding, knowing and coding is very easy. In addition, the concept of blocks does not include curly brackets, so indentation is compulsory. This also assists with the code's readability.

h. Object-Oriented

The object-oriented and procedural programming concepts are assisted by this specific language. Although this skill enables us with the reusability of software, classes and objects encourage us to design real life. A category allows tasks and information to be encapsulated into one.

I. Free and Open-Source

Python is easily available. Even though it can be conveniently installed at no expense; furthermore, you may also access and share the source code, make changes to it. It includes a huge library set to support you with your assignments.

j. Portable

When you develop your project in C and you want to run it on another platform, you may need to make some improvements to it, although this isn't quite the same with Python. You only need to write once below, and you may run it anywhere. Write Once Run Anywhere (WORA) termed this. Nonetheless, to avoid adding any system-dependent features, you must be vigilant sufficient

k. Interpreted

Ultimately, we have to assume it's a language that has been misunderstood. Although statements are implemented one by one, debugging is simpler than in the languages compiled

Disadvantages of the Python Programming Language

a. Speed Limitations

We also found the line-by-line execution of Python code. However, it usually results in poor execution because Python is interpreted. This, however, is not a problem unless speed is the project's emphasis. Simply stated, when speed is required, Python's strengths are adequate to outweigh its performance shortcomings.

b. Weak in Mobile Browsers and Computing

Although it can deliver as a great language on the server-side, Python is rarely seen on the client side. In contrast, it is seldom used to develop applications dependent on smartphones. There is a similar program called Carbonnelle.

Notwithstanding Brython's presence, the primary reason it's not popular is that it's not safe.

c. Design Restrictions

As you saw, Python is written dynamically. What this indicates is that when writing the code, you don't have to specify the type of variable. This uses the duck typing. Yet wait, what does it indicate? That just implies it should be a duck if it looks like a duck. However, during coding, this does not hurt developers but may rise runtime errors.

d. Underdeveloped Database Access Layers

The data source access levels of Python are somewhat underdeveloped when compared to much more famous technologies like JDBC (Java Database Connectivity) and ODBC

(Open Database Connectivity), As a result, it is less frequently used in large corporations.

SPECIAL OPTIONS THAT COME WITH PYTHON PROGRAMMING LANGUAGE

We would have around as many programming languages at a certain point in time as we could depend on our hands. A lot of programming languages are available in the market, and they come with their own unique features. However, its characteristics are what makes a language unique and finally, these characteristics are what determines whether or not the language will be selected for a specific task. Thus, we have to examine out the key features of python programming language before beginning with Python, which gives you explanations you should find out Python relative to several other tools or R.

EASY

Each time we talk about the word simple, we use it in different contexts.

a. Simple to code

It's very easy to code in Python, as we saw before. Similar to several other well-known languages such as C and Java, coding in Python is great. Anyone can learn the syntax of pythons in just a few hours. Mastering Python, though, includes learning all about its advanced stuff, as well as plugins and packages Which one is going to take time? It is therefore programmer-friendly.

b. Simple to read

Python code is written in English in order to become a high-level language. Looking at it, you can determine exactly what the code is supposed to do. Therefore, as it is dynamically typed, indentation is necessary. It assists in getting it understandable.

Read: Python Computer Language Development.

Expressive

Let's start by talking about expressiveness. Assume that we have two languages, A and B. Moreover, using community transitions, many applications that can be developed in A can be developed with B. However, you will discover many applications that can be created with B, but not in A, using local transformations. Python offers us many concepts that enable us focus on the answer rather than on the syntax. This is one of the exceptional python features that tell you to learn more about Python.

High- Level

It's a high-level language. This implies we don't need to know the system architecture as programmers, nor do we need to monitor memory. It will make it more programmer-friendly which is one of the key characteristics of the python.

Portable

Let's say you built your Windows machine's Python script. If you want to install it on a Mac, though, you don't have to make any changes to it. Simply stated, you can take a single code and operate on any machine. There is absolutely no need to create different codes for different devices. This makes Python a script that can be transferred. Nonetheless, in this example you must prevent any system-dependent functionality.

Interpreted

If you don't learn languages like Java or C, you need to compile it first, after that you run it. However, there is no necessity in Python to compile it. Internally, its source code is converted into a rapid form called bytecode. Then, all you need to do is run the Python code without caring about linking to libraries as well as a few other things.

By interpreting, it implies that the source code is executed one line after another. Because of this, debugging your code is easier. In fact, decoding makes it rather slower than Java, but it doesn't matter due to the benefits it provides.

Object-Oriented

It is assumed that an object-oriented programming language can simulate the actual world. It focuses on objects, functions, and data combination. Contrary to this, a process-oriented language focuses around skills that can be reused as codes One of the main characteristics of the python is that it supports object-oriented and procedure-oriented programming, in fact, unlike Java it supports most functions. For this type of item, a class is an approach. It is a knowledge that is hypothetical and has no meaning.

Extensible

You can write many Python codes if required in additional languages such as C, it renders Python an extensible language, that indicates it can be transferred to many other languages.

Embeddable

We just learned we could insert codes in Python source code in other languages. However, putting the Python script in a software program in an alternative language such as C is equally easy. This helps us to integrate scripting features into the other language of our software.

Huge Standard Library

Python includes a large library which you can use, so you don't have to write your own code for all of it. Libraries are present for regular expressions, image manipulation, email, CGI, databases, threading, web browsers, unit testing, generation of documentation, and many other features.

GUI Programming

To build quick GUIs, you can use Tk.

Dynamically Typed

Python is typed dynamically. This implies that at runtime the data type is decided, not in advance. Therefore, we do not need to define the type of data when declaring this.

WHY YOU SHOULD USE THE PYTHON PROGRAMMING LANGUAGE

One) Readable as well as Maintainable Code: While creating a software program, you have to concentrate on the quality of its source code to streamline updates and maintenance. The syntax rules of Python enable you to voice ideas without writing extra code. Python, unlike some other programming languages, emphasizes code readability, and also enables you to work with English phrases rather than punctuations. Hence, you can use Python to develop custom uses without writing extra code. The clean and readable code base will enable you to maintain and update the application without putting additional effort and time.

Two) Multiple Programming Paradigms: Various other contemporary programming languages, including Python also support several programming paradigms. It supports object-structured and object-oriented programming. Additionally, the language supports various concepts of aspect-oriented and functional programming. Also, Python also includes a dynamic type system as well as instant memory management. The programming paradigms as well as language features enable you to make use of Python for developing complex and large software apps.

Three) Suitable for Major Platforms as well as Systems At the moment: Python supports a lot of operating systems. You can also use Python interpreters to operate the code on specific tools and platforms. Additionally, Python is an interpreted programming language. It enables you to run the same code on several platforms without recompilation. Thus, you don't have to recompile the code after making some changes. You can perform the revised program code without recompiling, as well as examine the effect of changes made to the code right away. This feature makes it easier for you to make changes to the code without improving the development period.

Four) Robust Standard Library: Its big as well as strong standard library makes Python better than some other programming languages. The standard library enables you to choose from a broad range of modules based on your needs. Each module further allows you to add performance to the Python program without writing any extra code. For example, while creating a web program in Python, you can work with particular modules to implement web services, do string operations, manage operating system user interface or maybe hire web protocols. You are able to also collect information on the different modules by browsing through the Python Standard Library documentation.

Five) Many Open Source Frameworks as well as Tools as an open-source programming language: Python allows you to minimize software development costs considerably. You are able to actually utilize several open source Python frameworks, libraries as well as development tools to minimize development time without increasing advancement expense. You also have the choice to select from a broad range of open-source Python frameworks as well as development tools based on your needs. For example, you can streamline as well as speed up web application development with strong Python web frameworks like Django, Pyramid, Flask, Cherrypy and Bottle. Furthermore, you are able to accelerate desktop GUI program development by using Python GUI frameworks as well as toolkits such as PyQT, Kivy, PyGUI, PyJs, WxPython and PyGTK.

Six) Simplify Complex Software Development: Python is a multi-purpose programming language. Hence, you can use the programming language to build both desktop as well as web applications. Additionally, you can utilize Python to develop complicated scientific as well as numeric applications. Python was created with the option to facilitate data analysis as well as visualization. You can take advantage of the information analysis functions of Python to generate custom major data ways without putting additional effort and time. In the same vein, the information visualization libraries as well as APIs supplied by Python allow you to visualize as well as present data in an attractive and powerful way. Most Python developers actually wear Python to attain artificial intelligence (AI natural language and) processing of things.

Seven) Adopts Test-Driven Development: You can use Python to develop a prototype of a piece of software very quickly. Additionally, you can construct a piece of software from the prototype by simply refactoring the Python code. Python actually helps to make it simpler for you to perform testing and coding concurrently by adopting a test-driven advancement (TDD) strategy. You can quickly create the necessary tests before writing the code. It also tests the application code continually. The tests can also be used to check whether the application meets predefined demands based on the source code.

Python has Corporate Support. Do you believe that a programming language will become trendy just like that? No. Corporate support is a huge component of it. Lots of top companies, for example, Google, Quora, Amazon, Mozilla, Facebook, etc. use Python for their products. In reality, Google has basically adopted Python for a lot of its applications and platforms. Additionally, different tutorials and guides for dealing with Python are offered in Google's Python Class.

In a nutshell, a big part of the success as well as the growth of Python is attributed to the corporate support of several institutions that have devoted a good deal of effort and money to make the language better.

Python is utilized in Big Machine and Data Learning. Big Data and Machine Learning are probably the hottest topics these days. And Python is used in a lot of research as well as in the advancement of these fields. Python is essential in similar fields such as Artificial Intelligence. So it makes sense that this may be a big factor in the fast growth of Python.

There are lots of Python resources for analytics & information science like Scikit Learn, Theano, etc. Additionally, Python is utilized with great information with equipment including Pandas, PySpark, etc.

Python is used in Web Development and it is extremely well known in Web development. It's simple enough to learn but effective at powering several of the most favored sites on the planet, like Spotify, Yelp, Mozilla, Pinterest, Instagram, etc. (It is a win-win situation!!!).

There are lots of popular Web Frameworks in Python, which could be used based on the project needs. If the project is complex and comes with numerous requirements, it's safer to use a full-stack framework like Django, TurboGears, Pyramid, etc. But if the task is comparatively simpler, a microframework like Flask, CherryPy, Bottle, etc. can be used.

Python is utilized in Academics. When a language is presented in the coursework, it's arrived!

What this means is that Python is such an essential component of the programming community already. It's actually taught in colleges and schools as a primary language. This is because Python is mostly used in data science, artificial intelligence, deep learning, machine learning, etc. And since most of the students are interested in learning Python, it's obvious that its importance will increase.

Nevertheless, Python, like other programming languages, has its own shortcomings. It lacks several of the built-in features provided by various other modern programming languages. Hence, you've to utilize Frameworks, modules, and Python libraries to accelerate custom software development. Additionally, a few studies have shown that Python is slower than many popular programming languages, including C and Java. You've to accelerate the Python program by making changes to the application code or even utilizing customized runtime, though you can constantly make use of Python to accelerate software program development and simplify software application maintenance.

FASCINATING FACTS ABOUT PYTHON PROGRAMMING

1. Python was a pastime project

In December 1989, Python's creator Guido Van Rossum was searching for a craft task to keep him busy in the week around Christmas. He'd been considering composing a brand new scripting language that would be a descendant of ABC and in addition interest Unix/C hackers. He decided to call it Python.

2. Why it was named Python

The language's title is not related to snakes, but about the favorite British comedy troupe Monty Python (from the 1970s). Guido himself is a huge admirer of Monty Python's Flying Circus. Finding himself in a very irreverent mood, he called the task Python'. Isn't it an interesting Python truth?

3. The Zen of Python

Tim Peters, a significant contributor to the Python group, wrote the poem to spotlight the concepts of Python. When you import this into the Python of yours IDLE, you will find this poem.

4. Flavors of Python

Python ships in different flavors:

CPython- Written in C, most frequent implementation of Python

Jython- Written in Java, compiles to bytecode IronPython Implemented in C#, an extensibility level to frameworks created in, NET

Brython- Browser Python, runs in the internet browser

RubyPython- Bridge between Ruby and Python interpreters

PyPy- Implemented in Python

MicroPython- Uses a microcontroller five. Large Companies Using Python

Lots of big names use (or have used) Python for the products/services of theirs. Several of these are:

NASA

Google

Nokia

IBM

Yahoo! Maps

Walt Disney Feature Animation

Facebook

Netflix

Expedia

Reddit

Quora

MIT

Disqus

Hike

Spotify

Udemy

Shutterstock

Uber

Amazon

Mozilla

Dropbox

Pinterest

Youtube

What exactly are you watching for? Start learning Python today and build your career in it.

6. No braces

Unlike C and Java, Python doesn't wear brackets to delimit code. Indentation is necessary with Python. If you opt to import it from the __future__ deal, it provides you with a witty mistake.

7. Functions are able to return several values

In Python, a feature is able to return a lot more than a single worth as a tuple.

This is not likely in a language like Java. Generally, there, you are able to get back several values instead.

8. Python supports several assignments in a single statement

Python is going to let you assign exactly the same value to several variables in a single statement. It'll additionally allow you to assign values to numerous variables simultaneously.

9. You are able to chain comparison

Conditions may contain a lot more than one comparison at the same time. You are able to have an ailment that checks if a value is in excess of another and decreased than one more all at the same time.

10. String literals concatenate together

If you key in string literals separated by a room, Python concatenates them collectively. Thus, Hello' World' becomes HelloWorld'.

11. Antigravity!

When you reach the Idle and key in import antigravity, it opens a website with a comic about the antigravity module.

12. Python influenced JavaScript

Python is among the nine languages which influenced the style of JavaScript. Others consist of AWK, Scheme, Perl, Lua, Java, HyperTalk, C, and Self.

13. for and while loops are able to have else statements

The else statement isn't restricted to if and attempt statements. If perhaps you include an else block after a while- or for- loop, the statements within the else block are executed just after the loop finishes typically. In case the loop elevates an exception or even reaches a pause statement, the code under else doesn't perform. This may be very good for search operations.

14. _ gets the valuation of the final expression

A lot of individuals utilize the Idle as a calculator. In order to get the value/result of the final expression, make use of an underscore.

15. Folks prefer Python more than French

Based on a recently available survey, in the Uk in 2015, Python overtook French being the most widely used language trained in main schools. Out of 10, six parents preferred the children of theirs to understand Python over French.

PYTHON APPLICATIONS

1. Web and Internet Development

Python allows you to create a web application without an excessive amount of trouble. Its libraries for online protocols are XML and HTML, IMAP, FTP, e-mail processing, JSON, and user-friendly socket interface. Nevertheless, the bundle index has much more libraries:

Requests? An HTTP customer library

BeautifulSoup? An HTML parser

feedparser? For parsing RSS/Atom feeds

Paramiko? For applying the SSH2 protocol

Twisted Python? For asynchronous community programming

2. Applications of Python Programming in Desktop GUI

Many binary distributions of Python ship with Tk, a regular GUI library. It allows you to draft a user interface for an application. Aside from that, several toolkits are available:

wxWidgets Kivy? for composing multitouch applications

Qt by PySide or pyqt

And then we've some platform-specific toolkits:

GTK

Microsoft Foundation Classes with the win32 extensions

Delphi

3. Science along with Numeric Applications

This is among the common uses of python programming. Keeping its power in our mind, its' not surprising that python finds its place easily in the medical community.

SciPy? A collection of bundles for mathematics, engineering, and science.

Pandas- A data analysis and modeling library IPython? A strong shell for simple recording and editing of work sessions. Additionally, it supports visualizations as well as parallel computing.

Software Carpentry Course? It shows simple skills for systematic computing and operating boot camps. Additionally, it provides open-access teaching materials.

4. Software Development Application

Software developers use python as being a support language. They normally use it for management and build-control, testing, and also for many other things:

SCons? for build-control

Buildbot, Apache Gump? for automated and also constant testing and compilation

Roundup, Trac? for bug-tracking and project management.

Roster of Integrated Development Environments

5. Python Applications in Education

Because of the simplicity of its, brevity, and big community, Python makes for excellent basic programming words. Uses of python programming in training has a substantial scope as it's a fantastic language to instruct in schools or perhaps discover all on your own.

If you will still have not begun, we recommend you have a look at what we've to say about the dark and white sides of Python. Additionally, take a look at Python Features.

6. Python Applications in Business

Python is additionally a terrific choice to develop ERP as well as e-commerce systems:

Tryton? A three-tier, high-level general-purpose application platform.

Odoo? A management software program with a selection of business applications. With that, it is an all-rounder and forms a total suite of enterprise management applications in effect.

7. Database Access

With Python, you have Custom as well as ODBC interfaces to MySQL, Oracle, PostgreSQL, MS SQL Server, and some. These are ready for download.

Object databases as Zodb and Durus

Regular Database API

8. Network Programming

Along with those options, exactly how would Python slack in community programming? It can provide support for lower-level network programming:

Twisted Python? A framework for asynchronous community programming.

A user-friendly socket interfaces nine. Games as well as 3d Graphics

Safe to point out, this one is regarded as fascinating. When individuals listen to somebody's point of view, they are learning Python, the very first thing they get asked is? Have you produce a game yet?'

PyGame, PyKyra are 2 frameworks for game development with Python. Aside from these, we will also get an assortment of 3D rendering libraries.

When you are one of those game developers, you are able to check out PyWeek, a semi-annual game programming contest.

These are several of the main Python Applications. Apart from what we merely discussed, it nevertheless has many uses in even more places:

Console-based Applications

Audio? or perhaps Video-based Applications

Uses for Images

Business Applications

3d CAD Applications

Computer Vision (Facilities as color-detection) and face-detection

Printer Learning

Robotics

Web Scraping (Harvesting information from websites)

Scripting

Unnatural Intelligence

Data Analysis (Probably The Hottest of Python Applications)

CONCEPT OF PYTHON PROGRAMMING

Python is also offered with the earlier web development languages, produced by Guido van Rossum in the National Research Institute for Mathematics along with Computer Science in the Netherlands during the first 90s. The language borrows extremely from C, C, SmallTalk, Unix Shell, Modula-3, ABC, Algol-68 together with some other scripting languages. Rossum proceeds to direct the language development, although a principal development staff in the institute today maintains the vast majority of it.

As I mentioned before, English language keywords constitute the vast majority of the programming in Python. Just in case you learn them, most likely you have learned the majority part of Python. This can take a bit of practice, and you've to recognize the fundamental concepts before you start. Precisely why do not we begin by taking a glimpse at them:

Properties

Python is implicitly and dynamically typed, so you do not have to declare variables. The models are enforced, additionally, the variables are generally situation vulnerable, thus var, as well as VAR, are viewed as two distinct variables. When you'd want to determine precisely how any appliance work, you basically need to type the following:

Python does not possess the required characters to conclude statements. Any blocks are specified using indentation, so you indent to release a block & de dent to stop one. Statements eager for an indentation quantity ends with a colon. If you want to add comments, use the # sign for each line. Multi-line strings need to be used for multi-line comments. Values are provided using the = sign, and equality assessment is finished with two of them ==. You're competent to decrement or perhaps increment values with the operators = or perhaps possibly -= with the entire length on the right hand side. This may concentrate on some other data types as well as strings. You can additionally use several variables on an individual line, like so:

Data sorts Let's move ahead to info sorts. The info constructions in Python are dictionaries, tuples, and lists. Sets will likely be found in the sets library that is sold in many variants of Python from 2.5 onwards. Lists are for long one-dimensional array, although you can similarly have some other lists. Dictionaries are generally associative arrays, or perhaps hash tables. Tuples are one-dimensional arrays. Nowadays, Python arrays might be of any kind, together with sorts is certainly zero. numbers that are Bad begin out of the conclusion to the beginner, and also -1 is the last product. Variables likewise can lead people to works. Here is a great illustration of the usage:

You're competent to handle the colon to enter into array ranges. If possibly you head out of the novice index unoccupied, the interpreter assumes the initial product, consequently, the conclusion index assumes the last product. Poor indexes count out of the last item, therefore -1 is viewed as the last product. Here is an example:

In the last line, including about 33% parameter will watch the Python phase in the N goods increments, instead of one. For instance, in the above-mentioned examination code, the initial item is returned and after that the final, thus matters zero in addition to two in zero indexing.

Strings

Let us move onto strings. Python strings are competent to usually make use of single or double quotation marks, plus you're in a position to utilize quotation marks of only one type in a string using an additional kind, consequently, the following is valid:

This is a valid' string

Multi-strings are enclosed in specific or perhaps triple two fold quotes. Python has the ability to help support Unicode immediately, using the following syntax:

Flow management statements Python's flow management statements are while', for' and if'. For a switch, you've to use if'. For enumerating by show participants, use for'. For getting a choice checklist, use range (amount). Here is the declaration syntax:

range list = range(10)

>>>; print rangelist

[0, 8, 7, 6, 5, 4, 3, 2, 1, 9]

for quantity in rangelist:

if number in (three, 7, 4, 9):

break

else:

continue

else:

pass

```
if perhaps rangelist[1] == 2:

print The next item (lists are 0 based) is 2

elif rangelist[1] == 3:

print The next item (lists are 0 based) is 3

else:

print documents Dunno

while rangelist[1] == 1:
pass
```

Functions

The def' keyword is utilized to declare operates. Suggested arguments will be put in the performance declaration after necessary arguments, by setting the default values. Just in case of called arguments, the argument title is given a value. Features are able to get back a tuple, and also you are able to successfully return numerous values using tuple unpacking. Parameters are passed by reference, ints, but tuples, strings along with other immutable types are unchangeable as just the memory location of the product is passed. Binding another item on the adjustable removed the more mature one and replaces immutable kinds. Here's an example:

```
funcvar = lambda x: x one
```

```
>>>; print funcvar(1)

2

def passing_example(a_list, an_int=2, a_string=A default string):

a_list.append(A brand new item)

an_int = four

return a_list, , an_int a_string

>>>; my_list = [one, two, 3]

>>>; my_int = 10

>>>; print passing_example(my_list, my_int)

([1, 2, three, A brand new item'], four, A default string)

>>> my_list

[1, 3, 2, A brand new item ']

>>>; my_int

10
```

Classes

Python supports a really minimal multiple class inheritance. Individual strategies, as well as variables, may be declared with the inclusion of 2 or over underscores and a maximum of one trailing one. You are able to additionally bind names to category situations, like so.

category MyClass(object):

typical = ten

def __init__(self):

self.myvariable = three

def myfunction(self, , arg1 arg2):

go back self.myvariable

>>>; classinstance = MyClass()

>>>; classinstance.myfunction(1, 2)

3

>>>; classinstance2 = MyClass()

>>>; classinstance.common

10

>>>; classinstance2.common

10

>>>; MyClass.common = thirty

>>>; classinstance.common

30

>>>; classinstance2.common

30

>>>; classinstance.common = ten

>>>; classinstance.common

10

>>>; classinstance2.common
30

>>>; MyClass.common = fifty

>>>; classinstance.common

10

>>>; classinstance2.common

50

def __init__(self, arg1):

self.myvariable = three

print documents arg1

>>>; classinstance = OtherClass(hello)

hello

>>>; classinstance.myfunction(1, 2)

3
>>>; classinstance.test = ten

>>>; classinstance.test

10

Exceptions

In Python, Exceptions are managed by try-except blocks [exceptionname]. Here's a good example syntax:

```
def some_function():

try:

Ten / zero

except for ZeroDivisionError:

print Oops, invalid.

else:

pass

finally:

print We are completed with which.

>>>;some_function()

Oops, invalid.

We are completed with which.
```

Importing

In Python, outside libraries may be utilized making use of the keyword import[library]. For specific functions, you are able to use from [funcname [or] libname] import. Check out the following test syntax:

```
import random
```

```
from time import clock
```

```
randomint = random.randint(1, 100)
```

```
>>>; print randomint
```

```
64
```

File I/O

The Python programing language includes lots of libraries to start with. For example, here's a glimpse at just how we transform information structures to strings with the usage of the pickle library working with the file I/O:

```
import pickle
```

```
mylist = [This, 4, is, 13327]
```

```
# Open the file C:binary.dat for writing. The sales letter r prior to the
```

```
# filename string is utilized to avoid backslash escaping.
```

```
myfile = open(rC:binary.dat, w)

pickle.dump(mylist, myfile)

myfile.close()

myfile = open(rC:text.txt, w)

myfile.write(This can be a sample string)

myfile.close()

myfile = open(rC:text.txt)

>>>;print myfile.read()

This is a sample string'

myfile.close()

# Open the file for reading.

myfile = open(rC:binary.dat)

loadedlist = pickle.load(myfile)

myfile.close()
>>>;print loadedlist
```

[This', 4, is', 13327]

Problems, as well as variables Conditions in Python, is modified. For example, check out this particular condition:

One < a < three

This condition checks that an is actually in excess of one as well as under 3. You are able to additionally make use of del' to delete variables or items in arrays. A terrific approach to control and make lists is by show comprehensions, which happen to have an expression and after that a for' clause, followed by zero or higher for' or even if' clauses. Here's an example:

>>>;lst1 = [one, two, 3]

>>>;lst2 = [three, four, 5]

>>>;print [x * y for x in lst1 for y in lst2]

[3, 12, 9, 10, 8, 6, 5, 4, 15]

>>>;print [x for x in lst1 if four >>>; x >>>; 1]

[2, 3]
Check-in case an ailment holds true for any items.

any returns correct if any product in the list holds true.

```
>>>;any([I % three for I in [three, 4, 4, 3, 3]])
```

True

```
# This is because four % three = one, and one is correct, so any()
```

```
# return shipping True.
# Check for the number of products an ailment holds true.
```

```
>>>;sum(1 for I in [three, 4, 4, 3, three] if I == 4)
```

2

```
>>>;del lst1[0]
```

```
>>>;print lst1
```

[2, 3]

```
>>>;del lst1
```

Worldwide variables are called and so because they're declared outside functions and therefore are readable with no special declarations. Nevertheless, in case you would like to create them, you have to declare them at the beginning of the performance with the global' search term. Or else, Python is going to bind the item to a new community variable. Check out the test syntax below:

number = five

```python
def myfunc():

# This can print five.

print documents number
def anotherfunc():

# This raises an exception because the variable has not

# been bound before printing. Python sees that it an

# object will be certain to it later and also creates a brand new, local

# object rather than accessing the worldwide one.

print documents number

number = three

def yetanotherfunc():

worldwide number

# This will properly load global.
number = three
```

There's a great deal to python than what's mentioned previously. Of course, the main element to learning programming, particularly Python, is keeping practicing as well as testing. Python has a great array of libraries and great functionality you can discover and take advantage of. You can additionally find some other excellent resources and books to get more in-depth about Python. From classes as well as error handling to subsets and much more, the journey of yours to Python just started. There'll be syntax mistakes galore, but continue at it and use the exceptional Python community and information available, and you'll be fluent in it quickly.

USES OF PYTHON

Python has features such as high-level integrated information structures, strong typing, and binding, which tends to make it attractive for quick system growth. It is an open-source software and is rapidly available for use. Python makes debugging easy. For example, if the interpreter finds an error, an exception as well as stack trace is raised.

Python is considered an object-focused language. It's also known as a high-level programming language. It was created by Guido Van Rossum. It was initially introduced in 1991. The filename extensions are .py, .pyd, .pyc, and .pyo. It allows for straight and easy programming for every small and large application. It mainly focuses on code reusability, readability as well as using the white room. Python uses expressions primarily with the C language and its methods and typing. Python supports numerous programming paradigms such as functional, imperative, and procedural programming.

Python might be more user-friendly as a result of these benefits. Please find below the different applications of python language:

1. Applications:

Python is generally used to develop different programs, graphic computer operator interface-based applications, software development plan, as well as for scientific and numeric uses, network programming, games and other 3D and business applications. It creates an interactive interface, making apps created from it easy to use.

2. Multiple Programming paradigms:

Python is also used because it provides constant support to many programming paradigms. It supports object-oriented programming and structured programming. Python also supports many features of top-level programming languages. It is utilized in dynamic-type methods and instant memory management. Programming paradigms and python language features allow you to develop minor as well as large applications. It might be used to develop complicated software apps.

3. Robust Standard Library:

Python provides a big and strong typical library that can be used to enhance apps. Furthermore, it would make developers to utilize Python over various other languages. The standard library provides different selection of modules for Python. This particular module enables you to improve performance without writing a lot more code. To get information about several modules, refer to python standard library. While improving several web shows, putting on web services, performing various other string and usages businesses as interface protocol, the standard library documentation can be of great help to you.

4. Appropriate with Major Platforms along with Systems:

Python is compatible with great platforms and systems. As a result, it used largely for developing applications. Using python interpreters, python code might be operated on specific programs as well as platforms that support many operating systems, as python is an interpreter high-level programming language that allows you to run your code on many platforms. The completely new and modified code might be executed without recompiling as well as monitor or examine it. This shows that it is not necessary to recompile the code after every modification. This specific feature helps to improve the development time of designers.

5. Access of Database:

The use of Python also makes access to the collection easy. Python can be used to modify the interfaces of different directories such as MySQL, PostgreSQL, other databases, Microsoft SQL Server and Oracle. It is a product data source as Durus and Zodb. It is used in normal database API and totally free to download.

6. Code Readability:

Python code is very simple and easy to read and maintain. It can be reused very easily. Python has an extremely easy syntax, allowing different ideas to be created without writing any additional code. The code is of great quality, which is great. It is very simple to maintain the source code, which is needed to create the program. Furthermore, it improves code readability, which is a great feature, unlike other programming languages. It can also generate unpolluted code as well as customized apps for keeping and updating the system without extra work on the identical code.

7. Simplifies Complex Software Development:

Python can be used to simplify complex program development, as it is a general-purpose programming language. It is used for developing complex programs such as scientific and numeric programs, as well as desktop and web applications. Python can be used to analyze data. It also offers visualization, which could assist in creating custom apps without much effort and time. It allows you to imagine as well as present data in a great way.

8. Many Open Source Frameworks along with Tools:

Python is an open-source programming language. It is easily accessible. It also helps in costing program development significantly. You will find scores of open-source applications of Python frameworks, libraries, and development sources for enhancing the system without putting extra work. Python frameworks simplify and help make the job faster for web application development using frameworks such as Django, Flask, pyramid, etc. Python GUI frameworks can be used to enhance a GUI-based app.

9. Adopts Test-driven Development:

Python will make Positive Many Meanings - coding less complicated additionally to assessments together with the aid of creating the Test Driven Development technique. The test cases could be created before any code development. Every time the code advancement is started, the written test cases are in a position to start testing the code concurrently and also provide the final result. These may furthermore be utilized for checking or perhaps testing the pre-requirements based on the source code.

10. Various other applications that python is used:

In addition, python can be used in Robotics, web scraping, scripting, artificial intelligence, data analysis, machine learning, face detection, like detection, 3d CAD shows, console-based applications, audio-based applications, video-based applications, enterprise applications, together with applications for images, etc.

Python has capabilities that take good care of regular programming tasks. Python is quite simple to learn and really easy to use. Sometimes, python may be slower than other popular programming languages such as Java. Python programs can be accelerated by simply keeping the code and using customized runtime.

Many companies are using Python these days to perform considerable tasks. You don't get to find out about this because these businesses protect their trade tips. Nevertheless, Python makes a big impact on how groups perform. Below are a few primary ways Python may be utilized commercially.

Corel: PaintShop Pro is a piece of software many people have been using throughout the years to obtain screenshots, change images, draw new images, as well as perform a huge number of extra graphics tasks. The amazing thing about this software is that it runs basically on Python scripting. Put quite simply, to automate tasks within PaintShop Pro, you've to learn Python.

D Link: Upgrading firmware with a method link might be challenging, and D Link was encountering a circumstance wherein each improvement was tying up a machine - poor use of internet information. Furthermore, several upgrades require extra work as a result of the problems with the target device. Utilizing Python to create a multithreaded system to get content on the gear allows a machine to service a few items. In addition to a completely new strategy, Python cuts down on the number of reboots to only one, following the fitting of the completely new firmware. D-Link opted for Python instead of other languages because it provides an easier-to-use serial correspondence code.

Eve Online: Games are a major business since a lot of people enjoy playing them. Eve Online is a Massive Multiplayer Online Role-Playing Game (MMORPG) that relies a great deal on Python for the consumer & server ends of the game. It truly depends on a Python variant known as Stackless Python, which is vital since you confront these versions at all times with Python. Think of them as Python on steroids. These variants have the advantages of Python, along with several extra perks. The issue with this particular company is that using an MMORPG takes a substantial horsepower. In addition, the company wouldn't want to use Python except it truly needed it for the task.

ForecastWatch.com: If you have ever wondered if someone reviews the performance of the weatherman, look no further as there is ForecastWatch.com. This specific business compares the forecasts developed by a substantial amount of weather forecasters each day against genuine climatological details to discover how reliable these forecasters are. The resulting reports are then utilized to enhance weather forecasts. In this specific scenario, the software used to produce the comparisons is created with healthy Python since it provides frequent libraries useful in collecting, parsing, and storing information from online resources. Furthermore, Python's enhanced multithreading capabilities allow it to collect the forecasts from approximately 5,000 online resources each day. Most significantly, the code is a great deal lesser than what would have been desired by other languages like Java or Php.

Frequentis: The next time you fly somewhere, you will be based on Python being you on the floor easily again. It appears that Frequentis is the mastermind of TAPTools, a software package formula that is used in air traffic control in many airports. This particular unit provides updates on the weather in addition to runway scenarios to air traffic controllers.

Honeywell: Documenting large systems is error-prone and costly. Honeywell utilizes Python to do automatic testing, although it also uses Python to handle the cooperative setting between applications used to create proof for the apps. The conclusion is that Python helps in producing the reports that produce the evidence for the setup.

HP: Finding everything you need on a company network is tough. Numerous organizations implement a personalized research application or work with off-the-shelf applications to ensure that workers are able to obtain the information they need fast. In this specific scenario, the research plan began life as Infoseek, changed names to Verity Ultraseek, and also it's last identified today as HP Autonomy. The utilization of Python makes it easy to modify the internet search engine to meet up with certain needs. Furthermore, Python supplies softer multithreaded operation compared to some other languages, including Java.

Manufacturing Light & Magic: In this specific scenario, you will realize that Python is used in the development process for scripting complex, computer graphic-intensive flicks. Initially, Industrial Light & Magic depended on Unix shell scripting, although it had been found that this particular solution just couldn't provide the required results. Python was then chosen because it's actually an easier-to-learn language that the organization can implement incrementally. Furthermore, Python might be embedded in a bigger program process as it is a scripting language, whether the unit is created for a language like C/C+. It appears that Python can interact with other languages in situations where some other languages can't.

Philips: Automation is essential in the semiconductor industry, so imagine trying to harmonize the work of a lot of robots. Adhering to a number of fixes, Philips decided to use Python for the sequencing language (the language that directs what measures each bot should take). The low-level code is produced in C, which is still an additional motive to work with Python, since Python works well with C.

United Space Alliance: This company provides considerable support to NASA for a selection of projects, such as the space shuttle. One of its tasks is to produce Workflow Automation System (WAS), an application designed to manage NASA together with various other third-party tasks. The setup uses a central Oracle collection as a repository for information. Python was selected over other languages like Java and C since it provides powerful entering in addition to pseudo code, as syntax is also an interpreter. The result is that the software program works faster and each unit can be accessed very easily.

Python does support modules in addition to packages, which improves method modularity in addition to code reuse. Python increases effectiveness, which makes it the first choice for a lot of developers. It serves as a great learning curve, as it supports functional and procedural programming languages. It is an open-source programming language and might be freely distributed. The programming language is mainly selected based on requirements as well as compatibility with platforms and databases.

PYTHON WEB FRAMEWORK

Python Web framework is a set of packages or maybe modules that enable developers to create Web programs or services. With it, developers do not need to handle low-level details like protocols, process/thread management or sockets.

Python web framework is going to help you with:

Interpreting requests (getting type parameters, handling sessions,..) and cookies

Producing responses (presenting information as HTML and in other formats,..)

Storing information persistently (and some other things) Now, let us take a look at the most helpful as well as popular Python web framework to aid you with Web development.

Python Full-Stack Frameworks

A full-stack framework in Python is but one which attempts to provide an entire solution for applications. It attempts to supply parts for every level in the stack.

a. Django

Django Python is a framework for perfectionists with due dates. With it, you are able to build greater Web apps in a lot less time, and in a lesser amount of code. Django is acknowledged for the way it focusses on automating. Additionally, it thinks in the Dry (Do n't Repeat Yourself) concept.

Django was initially produced for content-management methods but has become to use for a lot of types of web applications. This is due to the templating of its, instant database development, DB access level, along with instant admin interface generation. Additionally, it offers a web server for growth consumption.

Giant companies that employ Django Python are Instagram, Bitbucket,, The Washington Times, Mozilla, Disqus, and Pinterest. Actually, when we think about the conditions framework' and Python', the very first thing that involves the minds of ours is Django.

b. TurboGears

With TurboGears, you are able to create a database-driven, ready-to-extend application in just a couple of minutes.

It's an MVC web framework with ORM with genuine multi-database help as well as help for horizontal details partitioning. Additionally, it features a widget phone system to simplify the improvement of AJAX apps. You might also install the template engine Kajiki of its.

TurboGears is a microframework plus a full-stack fix. Its PyPI offer is named tg.devtools.

c. web2py

With web2py, you are able to produce, deploy, debug, test, administer the database, and keep uses through the supplied web user interface. It's no configuration documents, and you are able to actually run it all a USB drive.

web2py utilizes the MVC built-in ticketing phone system to manage errors.

d. CubicWeb

CubicWeb is a semantic web program framework that includes a query language along with a choice view mechanism. Additionally, it features multiple databases, workflows, security, and reusable elements.

e. Django-hot sauce

Django-hot sauce is a general-purpose web toolkit that sits in addition to Django along with other frameworks. It's an active Pythonic API which will allow you to create scalable web applications with the WSGI 1.0 spec. Additionally, it offers indigenous bindings for any Schevo DBMS, ZODB, Durus, as well as Authkit tasks.

f. Giotto

A rigid MVC framework that absolutely separates Model, Controller and View components, Giotto ensures that designers, Web designers, plus sysadmins are able to work by themselves. Additionally, it includes controller modules that enable you to build applications in addition to the net, IRC or maybe the command line. These are all of the most favored Python web frameworks.

g. Grok

Grok was created on the existing Zope three libraries. It seeks to offer a simpler learning curve, along with far more nimble development expertise by emphasizing tradition over setup and Dry (Do n't Repeat Yourself).

h. Pylons

Pylons is a light Web framework aiming at rapid development and flexibility. With all the very best ideas from Ruby, Perl, and Python, it will make for a setup, but incredibly accommodating Python Web framework. With Pylons, Web development is easy, flexible, and fast. Pylons are made in addition to Paste. But after being merged with Pyramid to develop the Pylons task, it's in maintenance only condition.

i. Reahl

You are able to make use of Reahl to have web applications in clean Python. Nevertheless, you might work with, modify, or perhaps compose widgets in normal Python code. These widgets portray certain server-side and client-side behaviors.

j. wheezy.web

Wheezy is a little, high end, along with high concurrency WSGI net framework. The key features of its incorporate routing, unit update/validation, authentication/authorization, content caching with dependency, middleware, and much more. With these, we are able to build a modern, effective web.

k. Zope2

Zope2 is appropriately the granddaddy of Python net frameworks, it's been a family of networks. It's a web framework along with a general-purpose application server. Today, it's mainly used for CMS. We likewise have Zope3, which happens to be a standalone framework and a group of related libraries.

l. Tornado

While Tornado is not that famous, it's great with non-blocking I/O. You are able to scale it to deal with tens of a huge number of open contacts. It will make for an ideal framework for night polling, WebSockets, along with various other usages needing a consistent connection. Formally, Tornado only supports BSD and Linux OS (Windows as well as Mac OS X- just for development). Tornado finds the origin of it is in the FriendFeed task, which then belongs to Facebook.

Non-Full-Stack Frameworks in Python

A Python non-full stack framework is going to provide the base program server. This sometimes runs as the own independent process of its, upon Apache, or even in some other environments. Let us take a look at the most favored ones.

a. Python Bottle

Bottle is a fast and simple micro-framework you can use to create little Web applications. It offers request dispatching routes with URL-parameter assistance, key/value databases, templates, along with a built-in HTTP server. Additionally, it offers adapters for third party WSGI/HTTP-server as well as template engines. This is everything in one file; there aren't any dependencies except the Python Standard Library.

b. CherryPy

It's a pythonic, object-oriented HTTP framework. A web program driven by CherryPy is a standalone Python program that embeds its individual multi-threaded web server.

In a manner, CherryPy is a better way in between the problem and the programmer. Additionally, it supports many web servers like Apache, IIS, alongside. CherryPy is going to let you launch many HTTP servers simultaneously.

c. Python Flask

Like we have stated before, Flask is a microframework for Python. It provides a built-in development server, unit-testing support and. It's additionally completely Unicode enabled with RESTful request dispatching and WSGI compliance.

Flask is going to be useful whenever you wish to develop small, simple applications. With it, you are able to operate the database of yours however you like- with SQLAlchemy or whatever. A goof Flask case is it's utilized by Pinterest and LinkedIn.

d. Hug

Hug is of all the fastest web frameworks for Python. With it, you are able to build APIs. It supports numerous API versions, instant API documentation, and annotation powered validation. It's built-in addition to another JSON framework, Falcon.

e. Pyramid

In contrast to a couple of we described thus far, the Pyramid is a framework for big uses. It's flexible; a Pyramid web program begins out of a single file module and evolves to an ambitious task. You are able to say it makes real-world Web application development as well as deployment more enjoyable, predictable, and effective. In fact, Pyramid is a Pylons task.

f. Albatross

It's a little, supple Python toolkit that allows you to develop extremely stateful Web applications. Albatross deploys to CGI, ModPython servers, and FastCGI.

g. Circuits

Circuits are very much loved CherryPy but it is a very effective web framework to improve standalone multiprocess applications. It supports concurrency, asynchronous I/O pieces, and it is event-driven.

h. Falcon

A microframework for tiny programs, app backends, along with higher-level frameworks, Falcon encourages following the idea of REST. It's of all the fastest web frameworks for Python and it is utilized by EMC, Wargaming, Opera Software, OpenStack, Hurricane Electric, and some.

i. Growler

Growler is made in addition to asyncio, and it is influenced by Connect as well as Express frameworks for Node.js. When you need ORM or templating, you have to install it by hand. It handles requests by passing by way of a middleware chain.

j. MorePath

MorePath is a supple, model-driven web framework. It supports Rest, and focusses on extensibility and reusability.

k. Pycnic

Pycnic is of all the fastest web frameworks for Python for building JSON APIs. The framework is object-oriented, along with enhanced JSON APIs. It only has resources for producing Web APIs which depart a less heavy impact.

l. Sanic

Sanic is a flask like a framework, but it's rapidly. It supports asynchronous request handlers and also creates code non-blocking as well as fast.

PYTHON PACKAGES

From our computer systems, we store our files in the organized hierarchies. We do not place all of them in a single location. Also, when our application development, we split it into packages. In real-life projects, programs are far bigger than what we cope with within the journey of ours of learning Python. A program lets us hold identical modules in a single place.

Like a directory might contain files and subdirectories, a program may contain modules and sub-packages. We've been using modules a great deal in the prior lessons. Remember collections, os, and math? Those were all modules that ship with Python formally. We are going to discuss the difference between a package and a module in the next lesson of ours. But for today, why don't we dive into the realm of Python packages.

Structure of Python Packages

A package may hold various other Python packages as well as modules. But what distinguishes a package out of a typical directory? Effectively, a Python program should have an __init__.py file in the directory. You might make it empty, or maybe you might save the initialization code in it. But in case the directory of yours doesn't come with an __init__.py file, it is not a package; it's simply a directory with a group of Python scripts. Leaving __init__.py unoccupied is indeed a good process.

Check out the next framework for a game: Here, the root offer is Game. It's sub-packages Sound, file __init__.py, and Level, and Image. Sound, even more, has pause, play, and modules load, apart from file __init__.py. The impression has modules open, change, and near, beyond __init__.py. Lastly, Level has modules startup, load, and more than, beyond __init__.py.

How you can Import Modules from Packages in Python?

A Python package may have numerous modules. To import among these into the program of yours, you have to make use of the dot operator(.)

In the above-mentioned example, in case you would like to import the ton module from subpackage audio, we type the next in the top part of our Python file:

import Game.Sound.load

Note we do not type the extension, as that is not what we talk about the module as. The subpackage Level possesses a module named load also, but there's no clash here. This is since we reference the module by its completely qualified name.

To escape being forced to kind a lot each time we had to make use of the component, we may also import it under an alias:

import Game.Sound.load as load game

(If you are working the interpreter, you might additionally perform the following: loadgame=Game.Sound.load

This performs just as fine.)

Conversely, you can do:

from Game.Sound import load

However, if the Sound subpackage features a characteristic volume_up(), we call it this way: load game.volume_up(7)

If perhaps we shipped this way:

from Game.Sound.load import volume_up() as volup

We might call the function just, without having to use a complete qualifier:

volup(7)

But this is not advised, as this could cause names in a namespace to clash.

If you import a phone, just the modules immediately below it are imported. An import doesn't import the sub-packages.

>>>;import one >>>;one.two

Traceback (most the latest phone call last):

File<pyshell#488>, type one,
in<module></module></pyshell#488>

one.two.evenodd

AttributeError: module one' doesn't have attribute two'

Likewise note that in case you need to check where the Python packages of yours are now being created, the path of yours will look something like this:

C:UserslifeiAppDataLocalProgramsPythonPython36-32Libsite-packages

The best way to Design your Own Python Package Now, to probably the most fascinating part. As we said, Python bundles are only a dictionary with modules and sub-packages, and also an __init__.py file.

From the example of ours, This is the hierarchy we create:

Python Packages

The best way to Design your Own Python Package

This is what we've in evenodd.py:

```
def check():
a=int(input( 'Enter a number'))
when a%2==0: print("Even")
else: print("Odd") Also, we have each __init__.py clear.
```

Today, we import and put it to use this way:

```
>>>;from one.two.even-odd import check as check
>>>;check()
Enter a number7
Odd

>>>;check()
Enter a number0
Even
```

PYTHON FORENSICS

Analyzing and investigating to collect as well as protect evidence from a computing device is in the center of cyber forensics. This could be presentable in a court of law. With the wide applications of its, Python also finds a use that is good in digital forensics. With it, we are able to extract proof, collect information, plus encrypt passwords. It is going to help us protect the integrity of proof. In this particular tutorial on Python Forensics, we'll discover Naming Conventions, Hash Functions, Cracking an Encryption, Virtualization, Network Forensics, Scapy and Dshell, Indexing, Searching, Python Imaging Library along with Mobile Forensics with Detailed Explanation.

A quantitative method of the strategy of the forensic sciences, Computational Forensics(CF) will help analyze as well as resolve issues in different forensic disciplines. This is using computer-based modeling, analysis, computer simulation, and recognition.

On the foundation of style evidence, like documents, shoeprints, fingerprints, and tool marks, it uses a gamut of items, procedures, and substances. Additionally, it involves physiological and crime scenes, digital evidence, DNA and behavioral patterns.

We are able to use algorithms coping with signal and robotics,, machine learning, statistical pattern recognition, data visualization, data mining, computer graphics, computer vision, and image processing.

But how's it distinct from computer forensics? While computer forensics studies electronic proof, computational forensics deals with different kinds of proof.

Naming Conventions for a standard Python Forensics Application In order to watch Python Forensics suggestions to construct a simple program, we should stick to specific naming events and patterns. Check out the following table:

Naming Convention Example

Constants Uppercase; terms divided by underscores SPEED_LIMIT

Regional variable camelCase with discretionary underscores current speed

Worldwide variable Prefix gl_with camelCase with recommended underscores gl_maximumSpeed

Function PascalCase with suggested underscores; energetic voice ConvertToMilesPerHour()

Object Prefix ob_ with camelCase ob_mySpeedrecorder

Module Prefix _ with camelCase _ speed recorder

Class Prefix class_ with PascalCase; keep it brief class_SpeedSystem Think about a hashing algorithm to encrypt data. This is one way and also will take as input a stream of binary information. Today considering real-life situations, this may be a file or a password, or other or binary even kinds of electronic data. The algorithm requires- Positive Many Meanings - this particular enter plus creates a message digest(MD). These digests are distinctive, and no 2 inputs are going to generate the exact same. Have a demo:

```
import sys,string,md5

print("Enter complete name") line=sys.stdin.readline()

line=line.rstrip()

md5_object=md5.new()

md5_object.update(line)

print(md5_object.hexdigest())
```

exit This system uses the md5 hashing algorithm. It requires the full name of yours, encrypts it, and secures it.

Python Hash Functions

A hash feature maps a huge amount of information to a fixed benefit, right into a specified length. An input usually delivers the identical output. This is a hash sum which has a characteristic with specific info.

Because it's virtually impossible to revert a hash feature, you will seldom find a third party hit (like brut force) on it. This is why we additionally call it a one-way cryptographic algorithm.

Check out this particular code:

```
>>>;import uuid
>>>;import hashlib
>>>;def hash_password(password): salt = uuid.uuid4().hex
return                     hashlib.sha256(salt.encode()
password.encode()).hexdigest( )' :' salt
>>>;def  check_password(hashed_password,  user_password):
password, salt = hashed_password.split(' :')
return     password    ==    hashlib.sha256(salt.encode()
user_password.encode()).hexdigest()
>>>;new_pass = input( 'Enter required password')
```

Remember to enter needed password ayushi

```
>>>;hashed_password = hash_password(new_pass)
>>>;print('The string to shop in the db is :' hashed_password)
```

The string to shop in the db is:

b1076bdba4cd3f71b927a7d43b8c0c6b767cf0b310c2371a192572f7f
671f271:17de37c5292f4bbc88e74acca7cdefb2

```
>>>;old_pass = input( 'Enter brand new password')
```

Re-enter different password ayu1dolar1 hi

```
>>>;if check_password(hashed_password, old_pass):
```

print(You moved into the appropriate password')

else:

print(Passwords don't match')

Passwords don't match

This is the flowchart for this particular code:

In the perfect cryptographic hash function:

We are able to quickly calculate the hash value for any input

It's infeasible to generate the initial feedback from a certain hash value

It's infeasible to change the input without altering the hash value

It's infeasible to find two various inputs using the same hash value

The best way to Crack an Encryption found Python?

We need to crack the content data we fetch during evidence and analysis. Let us discuss some fundamental cryptographic terminology prior to that.

Plain text is the initial message in a human-readable format. Ciphertext is exactly what an encryption algorithm turns this particular pain text in. Imagine the Caesar cipher by Julius Caesar to preserve the secret copy from the enemies of his. Below, we consider each letter in the basic text and shift it 3 locations in the alphabet. It is going to turn every A to a D, each B to an E, etc.

The types of design evidence we use are:

Tire Tracks as well as Marks

Impressions

Fingerprints

We crack the vector information in such biometric details to obtain foolproof proof. Let us take a good example.

```
>>>;import sys
>>>;def decrypt(k,cipher):
plaintext='
for every in cipher:
p = (ord(each) k) % 126
if perhaps p &lt; 32:
p =95
plaintext = chr(p)
print(plaintext)

>>> cipher = input('Enter message: ')
Enter message: Ayushi

>>> for i in range(1,95,1):
    decrypt(i,cipher)
~
}
|
{
z
y
x
w
v
```

u

t

s

r

q

p

o

n

m

l

k

j

i

h

g

f

e

d

c

b

a

`

—

~

}

}~

|

|}

{

{|

z

z{

y

yz

x

XY

w

wx

v

vw

u

uv

t

tu

~

~s

~st

}

}r

}rs

~

~|

~|q

~|qr

}

}{

}{p

}{pq

|

|z

|zo

|zop

{

{y

{yn

{yno

~

~z

~zx

~zxm

~zxmn

}

}y

}yw

}ywl

}ywlm

|

|x

|xv

|xvk

|xvkl

{

{w

{wu

```
{wuj
{wujk
z
zv
zvt
zvti
zvtij
>>>
```

Virtualization

Emulation of Inforamtion Technology systems such as networks, servers, starage and workstations is called virtualization. It enables these tools to create a virtual system. These virtual systems gets help from the hypervisor.

Here we will see how we can use it for computational forensics:

We can use the workstation in a validated state for each investigation.

Attaching the dd image of a drive as a secondary drive on a virtual machine, we can recover data.

We can also use the machine as a recovery software to gather evidence.

This is how we can create a virtual machine using Python:

Step 1

Let's call our machine 'dummy'. Each VM shall have at least 512 MB of memory, expressed in bytes.

vm_memory = 512 * 1024 * 1024

Step 2

Attach this VM to the default cluster.

```
vm_cluster = api.clusters.get(name = "Default")
```

Step 3

Boot the VM from the virtual HDD.

```
vm_os = params.OperatingSystem(boot = [params.Boot(dev = "hd")])
```

We then combine all options into a VM parameter object. Finally, we call the add method of the vms collection to the VM.

Let's take an example.

```
from ovirtsdk.api import API #importing API library

from ovirtsdk.xml import params

try: #Api credentials are required for virtual machine
   api = API(url = "https://HOST",
      username = "Ayushi",
      password = "abc123",
      ca_file = "ca.crt")


   vm_name = "dummy"
   vm_memory = 512 * 1024 * 1024 #calculating the memory in bytes
   vm_cluster = api.clusters.get(name = "Default")
   vm_template = api.templates.get(name = "Blank")


   #assigning the parameters to operating system
   vm_os = params.OperatingSystem(boot = [params.Boot(dev = "hd")])
```

```python
vm_params = params.VM(name = vm_name,
    memory = vm_memory,
    cluster = vm_cluster,
    template = vm_template
    os = vm_os)
try:
    api.vms.add(vm = vm_params)
    print("Virtual machine '%s' added." % vm_name #output if it is successful)
    except Exception as ex:
    print("Adding virtual machine '%s' failed: %s" % (vm_name, ex))
    api.disconnect()


except Exception as ex:
```

The output:

Virtual machine 'dummy' added

Network Forensics in Python

Investigation can get harder in the contemporary Python Forensics network. Such as inside activities investigating, response in breaching the support, regulatory agreements validating, or performing check on susceptibility. Let's discuss some basic terminology for network programming.

Client- It's a part of network sytem that can runs on a workstation or personal computer

Server- It's a part of network sytem that can runs on provides services to different computer programs

WebSockets- It's a protocol between client and the server that runs over a specific TCP connection. It can be possible to send bi-directional messages between the TCP socket connection.

Using these protocols, we can validate information sent to or received by third-party users. While using encryption we should use a secure channel.

Let's take a look at a program that a client uses for handshaking:

```
>>> import socket
# create a socket object
>>> s = socket.socket(socket.AF_INET, socket.SOCK_STREAM)
# get local machine name
>>> host = socket.gethostname()
>>> port = 8080
# connection to hostname on the port.
>>> s.connect((host, port))
# Receive no more than 1024 bytes
>>> tm = s.recv(1024)
>>> print("The client waits for connection")
>>> s.close()
```

Output:

The client waits for connection

Before moving forward with the Python Forensics tutorial, you should read up on Python Modules.

Python Scapy & Dshell

a. Python Dshell

Python Dshell is a Python based forensic analysis toolkit. It is an open source toolkit which is developed and released by US Army Research Laboratory.

We have the following decoders in Dshell:

DNS: Extract DNS-related queries

reserve dips: Identify solutions for DNS problems

large-flows: List net flows

rip-Http: Extract files from HTTP traffic

Protocols: Identify non-standard protocols

You can access the cloned repository on GitHub:

https://github.com/USArmyResearchLab/Dshell

b. Python Scapy

Python Scapy is a Python based forensic analysis toolkit use to analyze the network traffic, you can brows it here:

http://www.secdev.org/projects/scapy/

Analysis of packet manipulation can be done by using Scapy. It also allow you to decode the packets of a extensive number of protocols. Contrasting to Dshell, it can deliver a thorough report about network traffic to the investigator. It can also use third-party tools or OS fingerprinting to plot.

import scapy, GeoIP #Imports scapy and GeoIP toolkit

from scapy import *

```
geoIp = GeoIP.new(GeoIP.GEOIP_MEMORY_CACHE) #locates
the Geo IP address
    def locatePackage(pkg):
    src = pkg.getlayer(IP).src #gets source IP address
    dst = pkg.getlayer(IP).dst #gets destination IP address
    srcCountry = geoIp.country_code_by_addr(src) #gets Country
details of source
    dstCountry = geoIp.country_code_by_addr(dst) #gets country
details of destination
    print src+"("+srcCountry+") >> "+dst+"("+dstCountry+")\n"
```

Output:

D:\Python code>python dshell.py

src INDIA >> dst USA

Python Forensics - Searching With a search term from the information, we are able to look for proof. With a little knowledge and expertise, we understand what you should browse in a file, and what you should search within files that are deleted.

Python will help us with this with the standard library modules of its. With searching, we are able to get answers to

questions like 'who', 'what', 'where', and 'when'.

Let's take a Python example to find a substring.

```
>>> s1="He came by for blood and milk"
>>> s2="blood"
>>> s1.find(s2)
15
>>> s1.find(s2,10)
15
```

```
>>> s1.find(s2,20)
```

-1

Python Forensics - Indexing In Python Forensics, with indexing, we are able to collect possible proof from a file, a disk picture, a system trace, or maybe a memory snapshot.

Through indexing, we are able to search a keyword, and also carry out interactive searching making use of the index to quickly locate key phrases. We are able to further put it to use to show keyword phrases in a sorted list.


```
>>> groceries=['rope','milk','knife']
>>> groceries.index('knife')
```

2

```
>>> groceries.index('rope')
>>> s1.index(s2)
```


Python Imaging Library

Both basic data structures as databases and complicated ones as JPEG pictures hold data. We are able to access the easy people utilizing very simple desktop programs, and the intricate people utilizing advanced programming tools.

Together with the PIL, we are able to process pictures when using the Python interpreter. It supports a gamut of file formats; obtain the supply files from:

http://www.pythonware.com/products/pil/

This is how we extract data from images:

Let's demonstrate this on an image of penguins.

Use PIL to open this image:

from PIL import Image

```
>>> im = Image.open('Capture.jpeg', 'r')
>>> pix_val = list(im.getdata())
>>> pix_val_flat = [x for sets in pix_val for x in sets]
>>> print pix_val_flat
```

This notes necessary points, including pixel values.

Output:

[255, 255, 255, 255, 255, 255, 255, 255, 255, 255, 255, 255, 255,
255, 255, 255, 255, 255, 255, 255, 255, 255, 255, 255, 255, 255,
255, 255, 255, 255, 255, 255, 255, 255, 255, 255, 255, 255, 255,
255, 255, 255, 255, 255, 255, 255, 255, 255, 255, 255, 255, 255,
255, 255, 255, 255, 255, 255, 255, 255, 255, 255, 255, 255, 255,
255, 255, 255, 255, 255, 255, 255, 255, 255, 255, 255, 255, 255,
255, 255, 255, 255, 255, 255, 255, 255, 255, 255, 255, 255, 255,
255, 255, 255, 255, 255, 255, 255, 255, 255, 255, 255, 255, 255,
255, 255, 255, 255, 255, 255, 255, 255, 255, 255, 255, 255, 255,
255, 255, 255, 255, 255, 255, 255, 255, 255, 255, 255, 255, 255,
255, 255, 255, 255, 255, 255, 255, 255, 255, 255, 255, 255, 255,
255, 255, 255, 255, 255, 255, 255, 255, 255, 255, 255, 255, 255,
255, 255, 255, 255, 255, 255, 255, 255, 255, 255, 255, 255, 255,
255]

Movable Forensics in Python although is considered nonstandard in electronic investigations, we are able to use smartphones to relieve the process of ours.

Through appropriate exploration in Python Forensics, we might look for received phone calls and phone calls made. We can additionally extract messages, other evidence, and photos. Let us observe the way to get by way of a lock screen to extract information.

In Android, we are able to utilize a PIN or even an alphanumeric password. This can be between four and sixteen digits/characters. The smartphone shops this within a file password.key of /data/system. Android stores a salted MD5-hash sum and SHA1-hash sum of this particular password. Let us try processing this.

```
>>> public byte[] passwordToHash(String password) {
  if (password == null) {
    return null;
  }
  String algo = null;
  byte[] hashed = null;
  try {
    byte[] saltedPassword = (password + getSalt()).getBytes();
    byte[] sha1 = MessageDigest.getInstance(algo = "SHA-1").digest(saltedPassword);
    byte[] md5 = MessageDigest.getInstance(algo = "MD5").digest(saltedPassword);
    hashed = (toHex(sha1) + toHex(md5)).getBytes();
  } catch (NoSuchAlgorithmException e) {
    Log.w(TAG, "Failed to encode string because of the missing algorithm: " + algo);
```

return hashed;

We cannot crack the working with a dictionary encounter, since the hashed password is in a salt file. This is a string of a 64-bit arbitrary integer represented hexadecimally.

PYTHON SOCKET PROGRAMMING

With Python, you are able to use an operating system 's socket assistance. This enables you to implement servers and clients for connectionless and connection-oriented protocols.

Think about a bidirectional correspondence channel. Its endpoints are what we call sockets. Sockets might speak within the following ways:

In just a process

Between operations on a single machine

Between operations on various machines

Python Socket Vocabulary

Let us check out all we speak about when we talk sockets.

a. Domain

For transportation, we use protocols as AF_INET, PF_UNIX, PF_INET, and PF_X25 amongst others. This particular family of protocols will be the domain.

b. Type

Communication between 2 endpoints might typically be of sort SOCK_DGRAM for connectionless protocols as well as SOC_STREAM for connection-oriented ones.

c. Protocol

This identifies the process used in just a domain name as well as sort. This is usually zero.

d. Port

Servers listen to one or even a lot more ports for customer calls. But what appreciates could a port take? A Fixnum port number, a program name, or maybe a string positioning the port quantity.

e. Hostname

A hostname is something that identifies a system interface. This may be a string keeping a hostname, a dotted quad address, or maybe an IPv6 address. This could additionally be considered a zero-length string, an Integer, or perhaps a string "<broadcast>".</broadcast>

We are able to implement a socket over various channel types- as UDP. and TCP We are able to additionally make use of the socket library to manage transport.

Read Python Modules Vs Packages

Python Socket Module

Let us very first import the Python socket component for this.

>>> import socket

>>>

Now, we can use the socket.socket(socket_family,socket_type,protocol=0) function to create a socket.

>>>
mysocket=socket.socket(socket.AF_INET,socket.SOCK_STREAM
)

>>> mysocket

<socket.socket   fd=1524,   family=AddressFamily.AF_INET, type=SocketKind.SOCK_STREAM, proto=0>

Here, socket_family may take one of the values AF_UNIX and AF_INET. socket_type may be SOCK_STREAM or SOCK_DGRAM. protocol defaults to zero.

Python Socket Methods

Now, we may call any of these methods on this object we just created.

a. Server Socket Methods

i. s.bind()

This binds the address to the socket. This address holds the hostname and the port number pair.

ii. s.listen()

This starts the TCP listener.

iii. s.accept()

This method passively accepts the TCP client connection, and blocks until the connection arrives.

b. Client socket methods

i. s.connect()

This actively initiates the TCP server connection.

And

c. General socket methods

i. s.send()

This sends the TCP message.

ii. s.sendto()

This sends the UDP message.

iii. s.recv()

This receives the TCP message.

iv. s.recvfrom()

This receives the UDP message.

v. s.close()

This method closes the socket.

vi. socket.gethostname()

This returns the hostname.

a. Examples-Server

Let's first try implementing a simple server.

```
>>> import socket
>>>
myserver=socket.socket(socket.AF_INET,socket.SOCK_STREAM)
>>> host=socket.gethostname()
>>> port=9999
>>> myserver.bind((host,port))
>>> myserver.listen(5)  #This asks for permission on Windows
>>> while True:
    myclient,addr=myserver.accept()
    print(f"Connected to {str(addr)}")
```

```
myclient.send(msg.encode("ascii"))
myclient.close()
```

b. Examples-Client

Now, let's try implementing a client.

```
>>> import socket
>>> s=socket.socket(socket.AF_INET,socket.SOCK_STREAM)
>>> host=socket.gethostname()
>>> port=9999
>>> s.connect((host,port))
>>> msg=s.recv(1024)
>>> s.close()
>>> print(msg.decode("ascii"))
```

Other Internet Modules

There are some other modules, now let us work with networks:

httplib, urllib, xmlrpclib- For the protocol HTTP, dealing with web pages, on port 80.

nntplib- For protocol NNTP, dealing with Usenet news, on port 119.

ftplib, urllib- For protocol FTP, dealing with file transfers, on port 20.

smtplib- For protocol SMTP, dealing with sending email, on port 25.

poplib- For protocol POP3, for fetching email, on port 110.

imaplib- For protocol IMAP4, for fetching email, on port 143.

telnetlib- For protocol Telnet, for dealing with command lines, on port 23.

gopherlib, urllib– For protocol Gopher, for dealing with document transfers, on port 70.

Exceptions Thrown by Socket Programming in Python

The socket module might toss among the following exceptions:

a. different socket.error

This represents a socket related mistake.

b. different socket.herror

This represents an address related mistake.

c. different socket.gaierror

This represents an address related mistake.

d. different socket.timeout

This happens when a socket times out.

PYTHON STATISTICS

p-value contained Python Statistics When talking data, a p-value for any statistical model will be the likelihood that if the null hypothesis is correct, the statistical summary is identical to or even in excess of the particular outcomes. This is additionally termed' probability value' or' asymptotic significance'.

The null hypothesis states that 2 calculated phenomena encounter no connection with one another. We denote this as Ho. or H One this kind of null hypothesis could be the number of hours invested in the office impacts the quantity of income paid. For a significance level of five %, if the p value falls less than five %, the null hypothesis is invalidated. Well, then it's realized the number of hours spent in the office of yours won't impact the quantity of income you are going to take home. Remember that p-values are able to vary from zero % to a hundred % and we create them in decimals. A p value for 5 % is going to be 0.05.

T-test in Python Statistics Why don't we talk about T-tests. Such an exam tells us if a sample of numeric details strays or differs considerably from the population. Additionally, it talks about two samples whether they are different. Put simply, it provides us the probability of distinction between populations. The test entails a 't statistic. For modest samples, we are able to use a T-test with two samples.

a. One sample T-test with Python

Let us try this on one test. The test is going to tell us whether the ways of the population and the sample are different. Imagine the voting populace of India and also in Gujarat. Does the typical age of Gujarati voters differ from which of the public? Let us discover out.

```
>>> import numpy as np
```

```
>>> import pandas as pd
>>> import scipy.stats as stats
>>> import matplotlib.pyplot as plt
>>> import math
>>> np.random.seed(6)
>>> population_ages1=stats.poisson.rvs(loc=18,mu=35,size=150000)
>>> population_ages2=stats.poisson.rvs(loc=18,mu=10,size=100000)
>>> population_ages=np.concatenate((population_ages1,population_ages2))
>>> gujarat_ages1=stats.poisson.rvs(loc=18,mu=30,size=30)
>>> gujarat_ages2=stats.poisson.rvs(loc=18,mu=10,size=20)
>>> gujarat_ages=np.concatenate((gujarat_ages1,gujarat_ages2))
>>> population_ages.mean()
43.000112

>>> gujarat_ages.mean()
39.26

>>> stats.ttest_1samp(a=gujarat_ages,popmean=population_ages.mean())
Ttest_1sampResult(statistic=-2.5742714883655027, pvalue=0.013118685425061678)
```

Today this importance of -2.574 tells us exactly how aberrant the sample hostile is out of the null hypothesis.

b. Two sample T-test With Python

Such an exam tells us whether 2 data samples have a unique means. Below, we consider the null hypothesis that both groups have identical means. We do not require a recognized public parameter for this.

Let us revise Recursion found Python

```
>>> np.random.seed(12)
>>>
maharashtra_ages1=stats.poisson.rvs(loc=18,mu=33,size=30)
>>>
maharashtra_ages2=stats.poisson.rvs(loc=18,mu=13,size=20)
>>>
maharashtra_ages=np.concatenate((maharashtra_ages1,maharashtra_ages2))
>>> maharashtra_ages.mean()
42.26
```

```
>>>
stats.ttest_ind(a=gujarat_ages,b=maharashtra_ages,equal_var=False)
Ttest_indResult(statistic=-1.4415218453964938,
pvalue=0.1526272389714945)
```

The importance of 0.152 tells us there is a 15.2 % possibility that the sample information is far apart for 2 the same organizations. This is greater than the five % confidence level.

c. Paired T-test With Python

If you need to examine just how various samples from the identical group are, you are able to go for a paired T-test. Let us take a good example.

```
>>> np.random.seed(11)
>>> before=stats.norm.rvs(scale=30,loc=250,size=100)
>>> after=before+stats.norm.rvs(scale=5,loc=-1.25,size=100)
>>> weight_df=pd.DataFrame({"weight_before":before,
                "weight_after":after,
                "weight_change":after-before})
>>> weight_df.describe()


>>> stats.ttest_rel(a=before,b=after)
Ttest_relResult(statistic=2.5720175998568284,
pvalue=0.011596444318439857)
```

Thus, we see we've just 1 % chances to uncover such large differences between samples.

KS Test in Python Statistics This is the Kolmogorov Smirnov test. It allows us to test the theory that the sample is a component of the standard t distribution. Let us take a good example.

```
>>> stats.kstest(x,'t',(10,))
KstestResult(statistic=0.023682909426459897,
pvalue=0.6289865281325614)


>>> stats.kstest(x,'norm')
KstestResult(statistic=0.019334747291889,
pvalue=0.8488119233062457)
```

Pay attention to the p-values in both cases.

a. Two samples

What we saw above was the KS test for one sample. Let's try two.

```
>>> stats.ks_2samp(gujarat_ages,maharashtra_ages)
Ks_2sampResult(statistic=0.26, pvalue=0.056045859714424606)
```

Correlation in Python Statistics This is a statistical connection between 2 arbitrary variables (or bivariate data). This may be causal. It's a degree of how close 2 variables are to keeping a linear relationship to one another. One particular instance is going to be the correlation between supply and demand for just merchandise whose supply is limited.

Have a glimpse at Exception Handling in Python Correlation is able to denote a predictive connection which we are able to exploit. In order to determine the level of correlation, we are able to create constants like or even r. The positives of correlation-

Predicting 1 amount from another

Finding the presence of a causal relationship

Foundation for some other modeling methods a. Instance of Correlation In Python

Let us take a good example.

```
>>>
df=pd.read_csv('furniture.csv',index_col='Serial',parse_dates=Tr
ue)
>>> df['Gross']=df.Cost+df.Cost*10
>>> df.describe()


>>> df.corr()
```

Python Statistics

Instance of Python Correlation

This will give us just how each column correlates to the next. You are able to additionally compute the covariance in the following way-

```
>>> df.cov()
```

	Cost	Gross
Cost	3.131608e+08	3.444769e+09
Gross	3.444769e+09	3.789246e+10

b. Plotting Correlation in Python

Let's use seaborn to plot the correlation between columns of the 'iris' dataset.

Let's revise Python Iterator

```
>>> import seaborn as sn
>>> df1=sn.load_dataset('iris')
>>> sn.pairplot(df,kind='scatter')
<seaborn.axisgrid.PairGrid object at 0x06294090>
```

```
>>> plt.show()
```

c. Saving the Results

We can export the result of a correlation as a CSV file.

```
>>> d=df1.corr()
>>> d.to_csv('iriscorrelation.csv')
```

WHAT IS PYTHON PROBABILITY DISTRIBUTION?

A probability division is a characteristic under statistics- one and probability theory that provides us exactly how likely various results are located in an experiment. It identifies functions in the terminology of the probabilities of theirs; This is out of all possible results. Let us take the probability division of a good coin toss. Below, heads have a value of X=0.5 as well as tails get X=0.5 also.

2 martial arts classes of such a distribution are continuous and discrete. The former represented by a probability mass performance as well as the latter by a probability density feature.

The best way to Implement Python Probability Distributions?

Let us apply these sorts of Python Probability Distributions, we need to find out them:

a. Normal Distribution in Python

Python regular distribution is a characteristic which distributes arbitrary variables in a graph that's formed as a symmetrical bell. It does so by arranging the probability division for every worth. Let us use Python numpy for this.

```
>>> import scipy.stats
>>> import numpy as np
>>> import matplotlib.pyplot as plt
>>> np.random.seed(1234)
>>> samples=np.random.lognormal(mean=1.,sigma=.4,size=10000)
>>> shape,loc,scale=scipy.stats.lognorm.fit(samples,floc=0)
>>> num_bins=50
>>> clr="#EFEFEF"
```

```
>>>
counts,edges,patches=plt.hist(samples,bins=num_bins,color=clr)
>>> centers=0.5*(edges[:-1]+edges[1:])
>>> cdf=scipy.stats.lognorm.cdf(edges,shape,loc=loc,scale=scale)
>>> prob=np.diff(cdf)
>>> plt.plot(centers,samples.size*prob,'k-',linewidth=2)
[<matplotlib.lines.Line2D object at 0x0359E890>]


>>> plt.show()
```

Binomial Distribution in Python Python binomial distribution informs us of the likelihood of how frequently there is going to be a success in n impartial tests. This kind of experiment is yes-no questions. One instance might be tossing a coin.

Let us check out SciPy Tutorial - Linear Algebra, Benefits, Special Functions

```
>>> import seaborn
>>> from scipy.stats import binom
>>> data=binom.rvs(n=17,p=0.7,loc=0,size=1010)
>>> ax=seaborn.distplot(data,
        kde=True,
        color='pink',
        hist_kws={"linewidth": 22,'alpha':0.77})
>>> ax.set(xlabel='Binomial',ylabel='Frequency')
[Text(0,0.5,'Frequency'), Text(0.5,0,'Binomial')]


>>> plt.show()
```

b. Poisson Distribution in Python

Python Poisson distribution tells us about precisely how likely it's that a particular number of incidents take place in a fixed interval of space or time. This assumes that these happenings occur at a continuous speed as well as free from the final occasion.

```
>>> import numpy as np
>>> s=np.random.poisson(5, 10000)
>>> import matplotlib.pyplot as plt
>>> plt.hist(s,16,normed=True,color='Green')
```

(array([5.86666667e-03,   3.55200000e-02,   8.86400000e-02, 1.48906667e-01,

1.91573333e-01, 1.81440000e-01, 1.56160000e-01, 1.16586667e-01,

6.65600000e-02,   3.90400000e-02,   2.06933333e-02, 9.06666667e-03,

3.84000000e-03,   2.13333333e-03,   5.33333333e-04, 1.06666667e-04]), array([0. , 0.9375, 1.875 , 2.8125, 3.75 , 4.6875, 5.625 ,

6.5625, 7.5 , 8.4375, 9.375 , 10.3125, 11.25 , 12.1875,

13.125 , 14.0625, 15.]), <a list of 16 Patch objects>)

```
>>> plt.show()
```

Bernoulli Distribution in Python

Python Bernoulli Distribution is a case of binomial distribution where we conduct a single experiment. This is a discrete probability distribution with probability p for value 1 and probability q=1-p for value 0. p can be for success, yes, true, or one. Similarly, q=1-p can be for failure, no, false, or zero.

```
>>> s=np.random.binomial(10,0.5,1000)
>>> plt.hist(s,16,normed=True,color='Brown')
(array([0.00177778, 0.02311111, 0. , 0.08711111, 0. ,
0.18666667, 0. , 0.33777778, 0.45155556, 0. ,
0.37688889, 0. , 0.224 , 0. , 0.07466667,
0.01422222]), array([0. , 0.5625, 1.125 , 1.6875, 2.25 , 2.8125,
3.375 , 3.9375,
4.5 , 5.0625, 5.625 , 6.1875, 6.75 , 7.3125, 7.875 , 8.4375,
9. ]), <a list of 16 Patch objects>)
```

PYTHON NOSQL DATABASE

From our last Python tutorial, we learned Python Database Access. Below, in this particular Python NoSQL Database tutorial, we are going to study the working of NoSQL Database in Python Programming Language. Additionally, we are going to discuss the necessity as well as the advantages of Python NoSQL Database. In addition to this will practice various kinds of different functions and NoSQL like how you can place into, upgrade, and delete information from a NoSQL database. We are going to use MongoDB for this. At last, we are going to cover the NoSQL vs SQL.

Thus, we need to have the NoSQL Database in Python.

How you can Handle NoSQL Database in Python applying PyMongo

What's the NoSQL Database?

Prior to beginning NoSQL Database in Python, we need to discover NoSQL.

NoSQL expands to "Not Only SQL". It lends us a means to keep as well as access information which we are able to model in forms apart from relational (tables). NoSQL databases mostly find the uses of applications involving big data in addition to real-time uses. The main reason we call them "Not Only SQL" is since they might help support query languages which are SQL like. We are able to make use of NoSQL to keep data in forms as key-value, columnar, document, and graph. When dealing with big sets of distributed information, we utilize NoSQL.

How you can Copy a File n Python Programming Language

Necessity for NoSQL Database in Python

Thus, so why do we need NoSQL?

Rather than big monolithic servers as well as storage infrastructure, organizations right now make use of commodity servers, open-source software, and cloud computing.

Tasks nowadays adopt nimble techniques rather than lengthy waterfall traditions (Agility).

There's a requirement to work with huge volumes of information which changes sort frequently. These kinds include unstructured, structured, semi-structured, along with polymorphic data.

The scale of audiences has grown exponentially through the years (Scalability).

Database Types with NoSQL

As we have reviewed previously, we've 4 distinct data types we are able to model with NoSQL Database in Python-

How you can Handle NoSQL Database in Python applying PyMongo

How you can Handle NoSQL Database in Python applying PyMongo

a. Document Databases

In a paper database, every important pairs with a booklet. A document is an intricate information structure and will store any of the following key-value pairs, key array pairs, nested papers. These store semi-structured information.

We work with these for applications as mobile application and content management data handling.

b. Graph Stores

A graph store holds information regarding data networks. One particular community is social connections. In a graph store, a node is as a history in a relational database, as well as an advantage is as a relationship between nodes. This allows it to represent information relationships better. We work with these for applications as CRM as well as reservation systems. Some examples are Giraph and Neo4J.

c. Key-Value Stores

A key-value store holds key-value pairs in the structure of its. This is the easiest NoSQL database. We work with these in use as session management as well as caching in web apps. Several examples include Riak, Berkeley DB, and Redis.

d. Wide-Column Stores

Whenever we wish to store columns together dealing with queries over big datasets, we are able to use wide column stores. We likewise discover these in SQL databases and query massive volumes quicker. Several examples are Cassandra, Google BigTable, and HBase.

Find out about Python Forensics - Hash Function, Virtualization

Benefits of utilizing NoSQL Database

This would be the coming benefits of NoSQL Database in Python, we need to talk about them one by one:

Simple and flexible object oriented programming.

Huge volumes of quickly changing data unstructured, structured, or perhaps semi-structured.

Scale-out architecture which is geographically distributed.

Agile sprints, regular code pushes, fast schema iteration.

NoSQL vs SQL

Thus, how are these 2 different? Let us find out.

Schemas are generally powerful for NoSQL but fixed for SQL.

NoSQL is able to have various types of database, as mentioned, but SQL has just one.

NoSQL came around in the late 2000s, SQL is hereafter the 1970s.

For SQL, the information storage model is single records, however, for NoSQL, this is determined by the database type.

NoSQL has horizontal scaling; SQL has vertical.

For NoSQL, advancement is open-source; for SQL, it's a combination of open-source and closed-source.

The NoSQL DB utilized decides assistance for ACID transactions; SQL supports ACID transactions.

Examples of NoSQL databases are HBase, Neo4J, Cassandra, and MongoDB; Those for SQL databases are MySQL, Oracle, Microsoft SQL Server, plus Postgres.

Installing the Prerequisites of NoSQL Database in Python

In this particular Python NoSQL Database tutorial, we utilize the library pymongo. It's the official driver posted by Mongo developers. You are able to put in it this way:

C:\Users\lifei>pip install pymongo

Collecting pymongo

Downloading
https://files.pythonhosted.org/packages/0f/54/ec07858c625460
027536aefe8bbe1d0f319b62b5884ec8650e1c2649dccb/pymongo-
3.7.0-cp36-cp36m-win_amd64.whl (309kB)

Installing collected packages: pymongo

Successfully installed pymongo-3.7.0

This installs edition 3.7.0, and that is the newest model of pymongo in the time of composing the tutorial.

You'll additionally need to set up the MongoDB database.

Stick to this link to find out much more about MongoDB Database

Python Interview Questions

Operations Perform in NoSQL Database in Python

How you can Handle NoSQL Database in Python applying PyMongo

How you can Handle NoSQL Database in Python applying PyMongo

a. Insert Operation

In order to place information to a NoSQL data source of Python three, we utilize the insert() technique. This is the code we utilize in the command prompt (You can also operate a script or just make use of the interpreter):

C:Userslifei> python

Python 3.6.5 (v3.6.5:f59c0932b4, Mar twenty eight 2018, 17:00:18) [MSC v.1900 sixty four-bit (AMD64)] on win32

Type assistance, copyright, license or credits for even more info.


```
>>> from pymongo import MongoClient
>>> from pprint import pprint
>>> client=MongoClient() #Choose client
>>> db=client.test #Connect to DB
>>> student=db.student
>>> student_record={
... 'Name':'Ayushi Sharma',
... 'Enrolment':'0875CS191003',
... 'Age':'22'}
>>> result=student.insert_one(student_record)
>>> pprint(student.find_one({'Age':'22'}))
{u'Age': u'22',
u'Enrolment': u'0875CS191003',
u'Name': u'Ayushi Sharma',
u'_id': ObjectId('7cyz7c2e72f5uh7829011e36')}
```

Have a look The Best Article on Python's Various Libraries

b. Update Operation

Now to update this data, we use the update() method.


```
>>> from pymongo import MongoClient
>>> from pprint import pprint
>>> client=MongoClient() #Choose client
```

```
>>> db=client.test #Connect to DB
>>> student=db.student
>>> db.student.update_one({'Age':'22'},
... {'$set': {'Name':'Ayushi Sharma',
.. 'Enrolment':'0875CS191003',
... 'Age':'23'}}) #Choosing the record to update
>>> pprint(student.find_one({'Age':'23'})
{u'Age': u'23',
u'Enrolment': u'0875CS191003',
u'Name': u'Ayushi Sharma',
u'_id': ObjectId('7cyz7c2e72f5uh7829011e36')}
```

c. Delete Operation

Now to delete this record, we can use the delete() method.

```
>>> from pymongo import MongoClient
>>> from pprint import pprint
>>> client=MongoClient() #Choose client
>>> db=client.test #Connect to DB
>>> student=db.student
>>> db.student.delete_one({'Age':'23'})
>>> pprint(student.find_one({'Age':'23'})
None
```

Here, Python prints None because it can't find that record in the database.

PYTHON DJANGO

Django is a high-level Python framework. It's open-source and free, authored in Python itself, and also follows the model-view-template architectural pattern. We are able to utilize it to improve quality web applications faster & much easier. Since developing for the net requires a set of the same elements, you are able to utilize a framework. This particular way, you do not need to reinvent the wheel. These activities include authentication, management panels, uploading files, forms altogether.

To serve a Request for a site We need to very first find out, in layman's terms, what occurs when the server of yours gets a request for a site. The request is passed to Django which attempts to evaluate the request. The URL resolver tries to match the Url against a listing of patterns. It functions this match from the best to bottom. If it is able to get a fight, it passes the petition to the view, and that is the associated function.

The featured view is able to check out whether the petition is allowed. Additionally, it generates a result, then Django sends it with the user 's web browser.

History

Adrian Holovaty and Simon Willison produced Django in the autumn of 2003 at the Lawrence Journal World newspaper

Django publicly released under a BSD license of July 2005; named after guitarist Django Reinhardt

Nowadays, Django is an open-source project with contributors across the world

MVT Pattern

MVC stands for Model-View-Controller. We make use of this when we wish to produce applications with user interfaces. MVT stands for Model-View-Template. A template is an HTML file combined with DTL (Django Template Language). Django handles the Controller portion, which happens to be the application code and regulates the interaction between another 2 parts View and Model. Whenever a user requests a source, Django acts as being a controller and checks in case it's out there. In case of the Url maps, View interacts with the Model and also yields a Template. Python Django sends back a Template on the person as being a response.

Find out about Python Decision Making Statements with Examples and Syntax

The unit will help us handle the database. View executes company reason and interacts with the Model to transport information. Additionally, it renders Template. Template manages the user interface and it is a presentation level.

The Model class holds important methods and fields. For every product type, we have a table on the website. Item is a subclass of django.db.models.Model. Each arena here denotes a repository field. With Django, we have a database abstraction API that lets us conduct CRUD (Create-Retrieve-Update-Delete) businesses on mapped tables.

Functions of Django

When dealing with Python Django, you are able to count on the following Django Features-

a. Scalability

If you have to scale the system of yours, you are able to merely increase the web nodes to the Django of yours. That's, you are able to scale it horizontally. 2 products that use Django's scalability are Instagram and Disqus.

b. Portability

The portability of Python makes for a transportable Django also. Different platforms include Windows, macOS, and Linux.

c. Security

Python Django ensures several arrangements for security also. One of those is the fact that it retailers hashed passwords in cookies.

d. Versatility

Python Django is going to work with formats like HTML, XML, JSON, among others. Additionally, it supports a number of different client-side frameworks. Thus, we are able to utilize it to construct anything including social networks and regular websites.

e. Packages

Django Programming has got the foundation of a huge number of extra packages.

f. Ease of Use

Features including the integrated admin interface allow it to be easy to construct with Django. It's additionally completely purposeful and finds it painless to swap databases.

PYTHON THREE EXTENSION PROGRAMMING

Python three extension Programming is some code which we write in another language like C, C++, or maybe Java Programming Language. We are able to import or integrate it right into a Python script. Thus, this particular tutorial is basically 1 on how you can compose as well as import extensions for Python. Extensions let Python speak with various languages.

The dll files (dynamically linked libraries) you might discover on the Windows of yours or perhaps the. Thus, files you see on your Unix are libraries. In effect, extension modules are libraries.

Structure of Python three Extension Module

A Python three extension Programming module is going to have the following parts:

Header file- python.h

An initialization functionality.

Features in some other languages.

A dinner table to map the names of the functions.

Let us look at every one of these by one.

a. Header File python.h

Let us write Python three extensions for C. Thus, we must include this particular header file in the C source file of ours. We place the include prior to all others. We likewise succeed this together with the Python functions we wish to call. This particular header file allows us to access the bodily Python API.

In the Python header, all sorts as well as capabilities start with the prefix' Py'/ 'PY'. For parsing information involving C and Python, we have the Python object pointer. This is the PyObject. Here is an example: static PyObject* myFunc(PyObject* self)

This header file also has some other functions:

PyArg_ParseTuple(args, format, ...)- This gets arguments from Python.

Py_BuildValue(format, ...)- This turns values into PyObject pointers.

PyModule_Create(moduleDef)- This initializes the module; wraps method pointers using module definitions.

For functions that return nothing, we use the value Py_None.

The PyMethodDef has the binding info. This particular framework ends with terminating NULL as well as zero values.

b. Initialization Function

If the interpreter loads the extension module of yours, it calls this characteristic. This is the final part of the Python three extension. You need to name this as following when you call your module' Sound', now brand this particular function' initSound'. It is going to look like this:

PyMODINIT_FUNC initModule() {

Py_InitModule3(func, module_methods, docstring);

Here, we have three parameters-

func- The function to export

module_methods- Mapping table

docstring- Comment

c. C Functions to Call

We can use one of three forms to return a Python object:

static PyObject *MyFunction(PyObject *self, PyObject *args);

static PyObject *MyFunctionWithKeywords(PyObject *self,

PyObject *args,

PyObject *kw);

stationary PyObject *MyFunctionWithNoArgs(PyObject *self); Whenever we make use of the Py_RETURN_NONE macro which the Python headers have to provide, we are able to possess a characteristic return None. This is the same as a void in C. These are static features. Here is an example-

```
static PyObject * module_func(PyObject * self, PyObject * args)
{
char * input;
char * result;
PyObject * ret;
//Parsing arguments
if(!PyArg_ParseTuple(args, "s", &input)){
return NULL;
}
//Running actual function
result=hello(input);
//Building a Python object from this string
ret=PyString_FromString(result);
free(result);
```

```
return ret;
}
```

d. Symbol/ Mapping Table

You need to register the function(s) in a symbol table for a module. For Python, all functions live in a module- even C functions.

This is a kind of PyMethodDef:

```
static PyMethodDef module_methods[]={
{"my_func",    (PyCFunction)module_func,    METH_NOARGS,
NULL},
{NULL, NULL, 0, NULL}
};
```

i. Parameters.

However here, we've four parameters-

Function name How the interpreter provides it; right here, it's my_func

Functionality address- Here, it's (PyCFunction)module_func

Flag- This may be of 3 kinds:

METH_VARARGS

METH_NOARGS- No arguments

Bitwise Or with METH_KEYWORDS For dealing with keyword arguments

Docstring- Whenever you do not wish to offer one, you are able to make use of NULL.

We terminate this with a sentinel keeping the NULL and zero. In the illustration, we've used NULL, o, NULL, NULL.

Setup.py Script

Right after composing a Python callable feature, registering it in the module 's sign table, plus publishing an initialization feature, we create a setup.py script.

from distutils.core import setup, Extension

#Extension module for C/ C++

extension_mod=Extension("hello", ["hellomodule.c", "hello.c"])

setup(name="hello", ext_modules=[extension_mod])

Wrapping

A wrapper is a characteristic which calls another. Below, a wrapper binds a Python item to some C feature. Let us see a few ways that are different to accomplish this. Up to now, we have just seen how to accomplish this manually.

a. SWIG

SWIG is an acronym for Simple Wrapper Interface Generator. While it supports a lot of languages, let's look at Python for right now.

i. A makefile

all:

```
swig -python -c++ -o _swigdemo_module.cc swigdemo.i
python setup.py build_ext –inplace
```

Read about Python Datetime Module with Quick Examples

ii. SWIG wrapper file

```
%module swigdemo
%{
#include <stdlib.h>
#include "hello.h"
%}
%include "hello.h"
```

iii. setup.py script

```
from distutils.core import setup, Extension
extension_mod              =              Extension("_swigdemo",
["_swigdemo_module.cc", "hello.c"])
setup(name = "swigdemo", ext_modules=[extension_mod])
```

b. Pyrex

Pyrex is a hybrid of C and Python. Let's try wrapping with this.

i. .pyx file

```
cdef extern from "hello.h":
char * hello(char *str)  #This takes the symbol 'hello' from hello.h.
def hello_fn(str):
return hello(str)
```

ii. setup.py file

```
from distutils.core import setup
from distutils.extension import Extension
from Pyrex.Distutils import build_ext
setup(
```

name="hello",

ext_modules=[Extension("hellomodule", ["hellomodule.pyx", "hello.c"])],

cmdclass={'build_ext': build_ext}

How to Import Python 3 Extension

You can import an extension like you'd normally import a module in Python–

import module_func

print(module_func.my_func())

PYTHON DATA CLEANSING

We will needtwo libraries for Python Data Cleansing - Python pandas along with Python numpy.

a. Pandas

Python pandas is an excellent program library for manipulating info and considering it. It will allow us to manipulate numerical tables in addition to time series dealing with information structures along with operations.

You're able to stick with it while using pip-

C:Userslifei&gt;; pip install pandas

b. Numpy

Python numpy is still another library we're planning to use right here. It lets us handle arrays and matrices, especially those multidimensional. Furthermore, it provides several higher level mathematical options to help us operate on these.

Use the following command in the command prompt to create Python numpy on your machine-

C:Userslifei> pip install numpy

3. Python Data Cleansing Operations on Data using NumPy

Utilizing Python NumPy, we need to produce an array (a n dimensional array).

>>> np.array([['a','b'],['c','d','e']])

array([list(['a', 'b']), list(['c', 'd', 'e'])], dtype=object)

>>> np.array([1,2,7,9,8],dtype=complex)

array([1.+0.j, 2.+0.j, 7.+0.j, 9.+0.j, 8.+0.j])

While dtype lets us tell the interpreter of the data type to use, admin, lets us define the minimum dimension.

The following parameters will give us information about the array-

>>> a=np.array(['a','b',2,'3.0'])

>>> a.shape

(4,)

>>> a.size

4

```
>>> a.dtype
dtype('<U3')
```

Let's Explore the Comparison Between Python Iterators and Generators

We can also perform operations like:

```
>>> b=np.array([[1,2,3],[4,5,6]])
>>> b
array([[1, 2, 3],
[4, 5, 6]])
```

```
>>> b.flatten()
array([1, 2, 3, 4, 5, 6])
```

```
>>> b.reshape(3,2)
array([[1, 2],
[3, 4],
[5, 6]])
```

```
>>> b[:2,::2]
array([[1, 3],
[4, 6]])
```

```
>>> b-4
array([[-3, -2, -1],
[ 0, 1, 2]])
```

```
>>> b.sum()
21
```

```
>>> b-2*b
array([[-1, -2, -3],
[-4, -5, -6]])
```

```
>>> np.sort(np.array([[3,2,1],[5,2,4]]))
array([[1, 2, 3],
[2, 4, 5]])
```

Python Data Cleansing Operations on Data Using pandas

Pandas use three types to hold data- DataFrame, Panel, and Series.

a. DataFrame

Pandas DataFrame is a data structure that holds data in two dimensions- as rows and columns. We have the following syntax-pandas.

DataFrame(data, index, columns, dtype, copy)

Now let's try an example-

```
>>> import pandas as pd
>>>    data={'Element':['Silver','Gold','Platinum','Copper'],'Atomic
Number':[47,79,78,29]}
>>>    frame=pd.DataFrame(data,index=['element    1','element
2','element 3','element 4'])
>>> frame
```

b. Panel

Pandas panel holds data in three dimensions. Etymologically, the term panel data from one source for the name pandas. A panel has the following syntax:

pandas.Panel(data, items, major_axis, minor_axis, dtype, copy)

```
>>> data={'Red':pd.DataFrame(np.random.randn(4,2)),
    'Blue':pd.DataFrame(np.random.randn(4,3))}
>>> pd.Panel(data)
<class 'pandas.core.panel.Panel'>
```

Dimensions: 2 (items) x 4 (major_axis) x 3 (minor_axis)

Items axis: Blue to Red

Major_axis axis: 0 to 3

Minor_axis axis: 0 to 2

c. Series

Pandas Series holds data in one dimension, in a labeled format. The index is the set of axis labels we use.

It has the following syntax-

pandas.Series(data, index, dtype, copy)

Let's take an example.

```
>>> data=np.array([1,2,3,3,4])
>>> pd.Series(data)
```

0 1

1 2

2 3

3 3

4 4

dtype: int32

Let's take another example.

>>> pd.Series(np.array(['a','c','b']))

0 a

1 c

2 b

dtype: object

Using these data structures, we can manipulate data in many ways-

>>> frame.iloc[0:2,:]

>>> frame.describe()
>>> frame.rank()

Python Data Cleansing

When some of your data is absent, as a result of any reason, the reliability ofyou're your predictions plummets. From one of our articles on information wrangling and aggregation, we discussed missing information and the way to minimize this risk. Let us find out how we are able to cope with this issue.

In real-time situations, in the comment section of our website. The email and name are necessary, though the entry for' website' may be left empty. Some users might not run a site to become eligible to fill in this specific info. In this way, we may wind up with missing data in several places. Exactly should we begin with this? Let us discover out.

Python Pandas is going to depict a missing worth as NaN, which stands for Not a selection. Just utilizing the reindex() strategy is going to fill in NaN for blank values.

```
>>>
frame=pd.DataFrame(np.random.randn(4,3),index=[1,2,4,7],colu
mns=['A','B','C'])
>>> frame.reindex([1,2,3,4,5,6,7])
```

a. Finding which columns have missing values

```
>>> frame=frame.reindex([1,2,3,4,5,6,7])
>>> frame['B'].isnull()
```

1 False

2 False

3 True

4 False

5 True

6 True

7 False

Name: B, dtype: bool

Ways to Cleanse Missing Data in Python

To perform a Python data cleansing, you can drop the missing values, replace them, replace each NaN with a scalar value, or fill forward or backward.

a. Dropping Missing Values

You can exclude missing values from your dataset using the dropna () method.

```
>>> frame.dropna()
```

This defaults to dropping on axis=0, which excludes an entire row for an NaN value.

b. Replacing Missing Values

To replace each NaN we have in the dataset, we can use the replace() method.

```
>>> from numpy import NaN
>>> frame.replace({NaN:0.00})
```

This way, we can also replace any value that we find enough times in the dataset.

c. Replacing with a Scalar Value

We can use the fillna() method for this.

```
>>> frame.fillna(7)
```

d. Filling Forward or Backward

If we move a method parameter to the fillna() method, we can fill forward or backward as we need. To fill forward, use the methods pad or fill, and to fill backward, use bfill and backfill.

>>> frame.fillna(method='pad')

>>> frame.fillna(method='backfill')

Python Data Cleansing – Other Operations

While cleaning data, we may also need to find out more about it and manipulate it. Below, we make use of some of these operations.

>>> data={'Element':['Silver','Gold','Platinum','Copper'],'Atomic Number':[47,79,78,29]}

>>> frame=pd.DataFrame(data,index=['element 1','element 2','element 3','element 4'])

>>> frame

"">>

True

>>> frame.head()

"">>

Data Cleansing Operations in Python

>>> frame.tail(3)

"">>

"">>

a. Renaming Columns

To rename a column, you can use the rename() method.

```
>>>                           frame.rename(columns={'Atomic
Number':'Number','Element':'Name'},inplace=True)
>>> frame
"<yoastmark
```

b. Making Changes Stay

Additionally, all through this tutorial "Python Data Cleansing", the adjustments that we've made on the frames didn't really alter them. To make this happens, you are able to establish the inplace=True parameter.

WHAT'S THE PYTHON REGULAR EXPRESSION (REGEX)?

Basically, a Python standard expression is a sequence of heroes, which describes a search design. We are able to subsequently make use of this pattern in a string searching algorithm to "find" and "find as well as replace" on strings. You would 've observed this characteristic in Microsoft Word also.

Python Regex - Metacharacters Each character in a Python Regex is possibly a metacharacter or perhaps a normal character. A metacharacter boasts a unique meaning, while a typical character matches itself. Python provides the following metacharacters:

Metacharacter Description

^   Matches the start of the string

.   Matches a single character, except a newline

But when used inside square brackets, a dot is matched

[ ]   A bracket expression matches a single character from the ones inside it

[abc] matches 'a', 'b', and 'c'

[a-z] matches characters from 'a' to 'z'

[a-cx-z] matches 'a', 'b', 'c', 'x', 'y', and 'z'

[^]   Matches a single character from those except the ones mentioned in the brackets[^abc] matches all characters except 'a', 'b' and 'c'

( )   Parentheses define a marked subexpression, also called a block, or a capturing group

\t, \n, \r, \f   Tab, newline, return, form feed

*   Matches the preceding character zero or more times

ab*c matches 'ac', 'abc', 'abbc', and so on

[ab]* matches '', 'a', 'b', 'ab', 'ba', 'aba', and so on

(ab)* matches '', 'ab', 'abab', 'ababab', and so on

{m,n} Matches the preceding character minimum m times, and maximum n times

a{2,4} matches 'aa', 'aaa', and 'aaaa'

{m}   Matches the preceding character exactly m times

?   Matches the preceding character zero or one times

ab?c matches 'ac' or 'abc'

+   Matches the preceding character one or one time

ab+c matches 'abc', 'abbc', 'abbbc', and so on, but not 'ac'

| The choice operator matches either the expression before it, or the one after

abc|def matches 'abc' or 'def'

\w   Matches a word character (a-zA-Z0-9)

\W matches single non-word characters

\b   Matches the boundary between word and non-word characters

\s   Matches a single whitespace character

\S matches a single non-whitespace character

\d   Matches a single decimal digit character (0-9)

\   A single backslash inhibits a character's specialness

Examples- \.   \\   *

When unsure if a character has a special meaning, put a \ before it:

\@

$ A dollar matches the end of the string

A raw string literal does not handle backslashes in any special way. For this, prepend an 'r' before the pattern. Without this, you may have to use '\\\\' for a single backslash character. But with this, you only need r'\'.

Traditional characters fit themselves.

Rules for a fight So, just how does this work? The following regulations have to be met:

The research scans the string begins to end.

The entire pattern must match, although not always the entire string.

The search stops at the very first fight.

In case a flight is discovered, the group() strategy returns the coordinating phrase. If it wasn't, it comes back None.

```
>>> print(re.search('na','no'))
```

None

Python Regular Expression Functions

We have a couple of functions to help us work with Python regex.

a. match()

match() takes two arguments a design and a string. When they match, it comes back the string. Better, it comes back None. Let us have a number of Python standard expression match examples.

```
>>> print(re.match('center','centre'))
```

None

```
>>> print(re.match('...\w\we','centre'))
```

<_sre.SRE_Match object; span=(0, 6), match='centre'>

b. search()

search(), like match(), takes two arguments- the pattern and the string to be searched. Let's take a few examples.

```
>>> match=re.search('aa?yushi','ayushi')
>>> match.group()
'ayushi'

>>> match=re.search('aa?yushi?','ayush ayushi')
>>> match.group()
'ayush'

>>> match=re.search('\w*end','Hey! What are your plans for the weekend?')
>>> match.group()
'weekend'

>>> match=re.search('^\w*end','Hey! What are your plans for the weekend?')
>>> match.group()
Traceback (most recent call last):

File "<pyshell#337>", line 1, in <module>

match.group()

AttributeError: 'NoneType' object has no attribute 'group'
```

Here, an AttributeError raised because it found no match. This is because we specified that this pattern should be at the beginning of the string. Let's try searching for space.

```
>>> match=re.search('i\sS','Ayushi Sharma')
```

```
>>> match.group()
```
'i S'

```
>>> match=re.search('\w+c{2}\w*','Occam\'s Razor')
>>> match.group()
```
'Occam'

It really will take some practice to get it into habit what the metacharacters mean. But since we don't have so many, this will hardly take an hour.

Python Regex Examples

Let's try crafting a Python regex for an email address. Hmm, so what does one look like? It looks like this: abc-def@ghi.com

Let's try the following code:

```
>>> match=re.search(r'[\w.-]+@[\w-]+\.[\w]+','Please mail it to ayushiwasthere@gmail.com')
>>> match.group()
```
'ayushiwasthere@gmail.com'

It worked perfectly!

Here, if you would have typed [\w-.] instead of [\w.-], it would have raised the following error:

```
>>> match=re.search(r'[\w-.]+@[\w-]+\.[\w]+','Please mail it to ayushiwasthere@gmail.com')
```
Traceback (most recent call last):

File "<pyshell#347>", line 1, in <module>

match=re.search(r'[\w-.]+@[\w-]+\.[\w]+','Please mail it to ayushiwasthere@gmail.com')

File "C:\Users\lifei\AppData\Local\Programs\Python\Python36-32\lib\re.py", line 182, in search

return _compile(pattern, flags).search(string)

File "C:\Users\lifei\AppData\Local\Programs\Python\Python36-32\lib\re.py", line 301, in _compile

p = sre_compile.compile(pattern, flags)

File "C:\Users\lifei\AppData\Local\Programs\Python\Python36-32\lib\sre_compile.py", line 562, in compile

p = sre_parse.parse(p, flags)

File "C:\Users\lifei\AppData\Local\Programs\Python\Python36-32\lib\sre_parse.py", line 856, in parse

p = _parse_sub(source, pattern, flags & SRE_FLAG_VERBOSE, False)

File "C:\Users\lifei\AppData\Local\Programs\Python\Python36-32\lib\sre_parse.py", line 415, in _parse_sub

itemsappend(_parse(source, state, verbose))

File "C:\Users\lifei\AppData\Local\Programs\Python\Python36-32\lib\sre_parse.py", line 547, in _parse

raise source.error(msg, len(this) + 1 + len(that))

sre_constants.error: bad character range \w-. at position 1

This is because normally, we use a dash (-) to indicate a range.

Group Extraction

Let's continue to start with the same email example. If you need to use the username only, then you can use an argument(like an index) to the group() method. Here is the example:

```
>>>match=re.search(r'([\w.-]+)@([\w-]+)\.([\w]+)','Please mail it to ayushiwasthere@gmail.com')
>>> match.group()
'ayushiwasthere@gmail.com'

>>> match.group(1)
'ayushiwasthere'

>>> match.group(2)
'gmail'

>>> match.group(3)
'com'
```

Parentheses let you extract the parts you want. Note that for this, we divided the pattern into groups using parentheses:

r'([\w.-]+)@([\w-]+)\.([\w]+)'

Python findall()

Above, we saw that Python regex search() stops at the first match. But Python findall() returns a list of all matches found.

>>> match=re.findall(r'advi[cs]e','I could advise you on your poem, but you would disparage my advice')

We can then iterate on it.

>>> for i in match:
    print(i)
advise

advice

>>> type(match)
<class 'list'>

findall() with Files

We have worked with files, and we know how to read and write to them. Why not make life easier by using Python findall() with files? We'll first use the os module to get to the desktop. Let's see.

>>> import os

>>> os.chdir('C:\\Users\\lifei\\Desktop')

>>> f=open('Today.txt')

findall() with Groups

We saw how we can divide a pattern into groups using parentheses. Watch what happens when we call Python Regex findall().

```
>>> match=re.findall(r'([\w]+)\s([\w]+)','Ayushi Sharma, Fluffy
Sharma, Leo Sharma, Candy Sharma')
>>> for i in match:
  print(i)
```
('Ayushi', 'Sharma')

('Fluffy', 'Sharma')

('Leo', 'Sharma')

('Candy', 'Sharma')

Python Regex Options

The functions we discussed may take an optional argument as well.
These options are:

a. Python Regular Expression IGNORECASE

This Python Regex ignores the matching case.

Let's see an example of Python Regex IGNORECASE:

```
>>>      match=re.findall(r'hi','Hi,      did      you      ship      it,
Hillary?',re.IGNORECASE)
>>> for i in match:
    print(i)
```
Hi

hi

Hi

b. Python MULTILINE

Python MULTILINE works with a string of multiple lines, this
allows ^ and $ to match the start and end of each line, not just the
whole string.

```
>>> match=re.findall(r'^Hi','Hi, did you ship it, Hillary?\nNo, I
didn\'t, but Hi',re.MULTILINE)
```

```
>>> for i in match:
    print(i)
Hi
```

c. Python DOTALL

Python DOTALL does not scan all in a multiline string; it only matches the first line. This is because . does not match a newline. To allow this, we use DOTALL.

```
>>> match=re.findall(r'.*','Hi, did you ship it, Hillary?\nNo, I didn\'t, but Hi',re.DOTALL)
>>> for i in match:
    print(i)
Hi, did you ship it, Hillary?
```

No, I didn't, but Hi

Greedy vs Non-Greedy

The metacharacters *, +, and ? are greedy. This means that they keep searching. Let's take an example.

```
>>> match=re.findall(r'(<.*>)','<em>Strong</em> <i>Italic</i>')
>>> for i in match:
    print(i)
<em>
```

</em>

```
<i>

</i>
```

This gave us the whole string, because it greedily keeps searching. What if we just want the opening and closing tags? Look:

```
print(i)
```

```
>>>match=re.findall(r'(<.*?>)','<em>Strong</em>
<i>Italic</i>')
>>> for i in match:
    print(i)
<em>

</em>

<i>

</i>
```

The .* is greedy, and the ? makes it non-greedy.

Alternatively, we could also do this:

```
>>>match=re.findall(r'</?\w+>','<em>Strong</em>
<i>Italic</i>')
>>> for i in match:
    print(i)
```

Here's another example:

```
>>> match=re.findall('(a*?)b','aaabbc')
>>> for i in match:
    print(i)
aaa
```

Here, the? makes * non-greedy. Also, if we would have skipped the b after the ?, it would have returned an empty string. The ? here needs a character after it to stop at. This works for all three- *?, +?, and ??.

Similarly, {m,n}? makes it non-greedy, and matches as few occurrences as possible.

Substitution

We can use the sub() function to substitute the part of a string with another. sub() takes three arguments- pattern, substring, and string.

```
>>> re.sub('^a','an','a apple')
'an apple'
```

Below, we utilized so it will not alter apple to anpple. The grammar police approve.

Python Regex Applications

They find take in these places:

Search engines

Locate as well as Replace dialogues of word processor as well as text editors

Text processing utilities such as sed and AWK

Lexical analysis

PYTHON COMPILERS AND INTERPRETERS

You might have read that Python is an interpreted language. Effectively, this is how it works.

A compiler changes the, py supply file into a pyc bytecode for the Python virtual device.

A Python interpreter executes this bytecode on the virtual device.

Let us look at what compilers as well as interpreters are out there for Python.

CPython

This is the default and most widely used implementation of Python and it is written in C. This is an interpreter and has a different interface function with languages as C. Here is a brief on it-

Developers- Python code developers, the Python group Stable Release 3.6.5; March 2018 as well as 2.7.15; May 2018

Written in C

Type- Python programming language interpreter

a. Style of CPython

Each CPython interpreter for Python, the task utilizes a GIL(Global Interpreter Lock). This can be considered as a limitation as it disables concurrent Python threads for a procedure. One other issue is the fact that to attain concurrency, you have to manage separate CPython interpreter operations with a multitasking OS. This causes it to be more difficult for concurrent CPython tasks to communicate.

Jython

Jython is JPython's successor. It's an implementation of Python which uses the Java platform. Here is a brief-

First Release January 2001 Stable Release July 2017, version 2.7.1

Written in Python programming, Java

Type- Python programming language interpreter

Jython requires Python code and also compiles it to Java bytecode. What this means is we are able to perform Python on any device which operates a JVM (Java Virtual Machine). Jython supports static as well as dynamic compilation and we need to extend Java courses.

IronPython

This is a Python implementation within the NET Mono and Framework. Here is a brief:

Author- Jim Hugunin

First Release September 2006 Stable Release February 2018; model 2.7.8

Written in C#

Type- Python programming language implementation IronPython supports powerful compilation as well as an interactive system. Python scripts are able to interact with, NET items.

ActivePython

ActivePython is a Python division from ActiveState. It makes installation simple and cross-platform compatibility attainable.

Aside from the standard libraries, it's a number of different modules.

Nuitka

Nuitka, source-to-source Python compilers that use Python code and also compiles it to C/C++ executables or maybe source code. Let us go for a brief:

Developers- Kay Hayen, others Stable Release October 2017; model 0.5.28

Type- source-to-source compiler Even if you do not run Python on the machine of yours, you are able to create standalone plans with Nuitka.

PyJS

PyJS is an online application framework that is going to let you make use of Python to develop client side web as well as desktop applications. You are able to run such an application at an internet browser and as a standalone desktop program.

Let us go for a brief:

Author- James Tauber

First Release March 2007 Stable Release May 2012; model 0.8.1

Written in Python, JavaScript Earlier, it was named Pyjamas. It translates the Python code of yours into JavaScript to allow it to run in an internet browser. PyJS ships with an AJAX framework along with a Widget Set API.

Stackless Python

Stackless Python is a Python interpreter. It is' stackless' since it does not rely on the C call because of its stack. It uses the C stack and also clears it between calls.

Here is a brief:

Author- Christian Tismer

First Release 1998 Stable Release September 2017; 3.5.4-SLP

Written in C, Python

Type- Interpreter

Stackless Python also supports micro threads and threads. Besides that, it offers tasklets, serialization, round-robin scheduling, and pre-compiled binaries.

WHAT IS PYTHON ZIP FILE?

Python ZIPfile is a superb tool use to combine the associated files and compress big files to reduce their dimensions. The compression is lossless. What does this means is the fact that using the compression algorithm, we're able to operate on the compressed info to flawlessly reconstruct the original information. So, in Python zip file is an archive information structure in addition to a compression standard; it has one particular file which keeps compressed files.

The positives of Python Zip files

Bunching documents into zip files are having following advantages:

1. It reduces storage room requirements, since ZIP data utilize compression, they are able to keep more precisely and exactly the same quantity of storage.

2. It improves the transfer velocity of normal connections, as it is basically one file keeping considerably less storage, it transfers faster

Python Zip file Module

The Python zipfile element has ability to produce, read, write, append, as well as capture ZIP files. At the time of posting. It allows us to deal with ZIP information which employs ZIP64 extensions and decrypt encrypted files in ZIP archives. It cannot handle multi-disk ZIP data or build encrypted data.

Python Zip file Module seems to have the following members:

a. exception zip file. BadZipFile

For a terrible ZIP file, it raises the different.

b. exception zip file.BadZipfile

This is an alias for the prior exception in the summary. It's making it suitable with more mature Python versions. This's deprecated since model 3.2.

c. exception zip file.LargeZipFile

Whenever a Python ZIPfile requires ZIP64 performance, though it has not been enabled, Python throws the different.

d. category zip file.ZipFile

This's the category for reading and writing ZIP documents in Python.

e. category zip file.PyZipFile

This particular category lets us write ZIP archives positioning Python libraries.

f. category zipfile.ZipInfo (filename= 'NoName', 0, 0, 1, 1, date_time=(1980, 0))

With this particular category, we are able to represent info about an archive member. The get info() as well as information list() techniques of Python ZipFile objects return situations from this category.

g. zipfile.is_zipfile(filename)

This considers the secret quantity of a ZIP file. If it's a legitimate ZIP file, it comes back True; or else, False. This works on documents and file like objects.

h. zip file.ZIP_STORED

This's the numeric constant for uncompressed archive participants.

i. zip file.ZIP_DEFLATED

This's the numeric constant for the typical ZIP compression technique. It requires the zlib component.

j. zipfile.ZIP_BZIP2

This's the numeric constant for the BZIP2 compression technique. It requires the bz2 module.

k. zip file.ZIP_LZMA

This's the numeric constant for the LZMA compression technique. It requires the lzma module.

5. Python ZipFile Objects

Python zipfile type this type:

a. category zip file.ZipFile(file, mode='r', compression=ZIP_STORED, allowZip64=True)

This technique opens a Python zip file. At this point, the file might be a file like an item or maybe a string road to a file. We have the following modes:

r'- To see a current file

w'- To truncate as well as write a brand new file

a'- To tack to a current file

Utilizing the compression argument, we are able to choose the compression technique to work with when writing the archive. allowZip64 holds true by default. This creates ZIP data which use ZIP64 extensions for zip documents larger compared to GiB.

ZipFile has the following functions:

i. ZipFile.close()

This shuts the archive file. When we don't call this prior to exit the software, Python does not write the records meant to.

b. ZipFile.getinfo(name)

This goes back to a ZipInfo item keeping info regarding the archive member name.

c. ZipFile.infolist()

This returns a listing keeping a ZipInfo object for every archive member.

d. ZipFile.namelist()

This returns a listing of archive participants by name.

e. ZipFile.open(name, mode='r', pwd=None)

This particular feature extracts a part from the archive to be a file like object (CipExtFile). The method is r', U', or maybe rU'. PWD could be the password for an encrypted file. the title is a filename in the archive or maybe a ZipInfo object.

Because it's likewise a context supervisor, we are able to utilize it with the with' statement:

with ZipFile(spam.zip') as my zip:

with myzip.open(eggs.txt') as myfile:

print(myfile.read())

f. ZipFile.extract(member, path=None, pwd=None)

This extracts a part from the archive on the present performing directory. member can be a filename or maybe a ZipInfo object, course is a unique directory to acquire to, and also PWD could be the password for an encrypted file.

g. ZipFile.extractall(path=None, members=None, pwd=None)

This extracts all people from the archive on the present working directory. The arguments suggest exactly the same as above.

h. ZipFile.printdir()

This can print a table of contents because of the archive to sys.stdout.

i. ZipFile.setpassword(pwd)

This sets PWD as the default password to acquire encrypted data.

j. ZipFile.read(name, pwd=None)

This comes back to the bytes of title in the archive, in which title will be the title of a file in the archive, or even of any ZipFile object.

k. ZipFile.testzip()

This determines the CRCs as well as file headers for those documents in the archive and also returns the title of the very first negative file. When there's not one, it comes back None.

l. ZipFile.write(filename, arcname=None, compress_type=None)

This creates the file filename to the archive, calling it arc name.

m. ZipFile.writestr(zinfo_or_arcname, bytes[, compress_type])

This creates the string bytes to the archive

We likewise have a number of data attributes:

ZipFile.debug

This denotes the degree of debug paper to use. zero means no output (default) and three means probably the most output.

ZipFile.comment

This's the comment text associated with a Python zip file.

The best way to Write Python ZIP File?

We utilize the write() technique to create to a ZIP. Here is the code we use:

```
>>>; from zipfile import ZipFile
>>>; import os >>>;os.chdir( 'C:UserslifeiDesktop')
> > >
>>>; def get_paths(directory):
paths=[] for root, directories, documents in os.walk(directory):
for filename of files: filepath=os.path.join(root,filename)
paths.append(filepath)
go back paths
>>>; directory= './Demo'
>>>; paths=get_paths(directory)
>>>; print("Zipping these files:")
```

Zipping these files:

```
>>>; for file in paths:
print(file),/Demo1.txt
,/Demo2.txt
,/Demo3.txt
>>>; with ZipFile( 'Demo.zip','w') as zip:
for file of paths: zip.write(file)
>>>; print("Zip successful")
Zip successful
```

Today let's see exactly how this works: We build a characteristic with uses the technique os.walk(). In each and every iteration, it appends the documents in that directory on the list paths. Next, we get a summary of the file paths bypassing the Demo directory's road on the performance get_paths(). Next, we produce a ZipFile object in WRITE mode. Lastly, we utilize the write() technique to create all these documents to the ZIP.

Obtaining Information regarding ZIP Files in Python

To discover more about a Python zipfile, we utilize the technique infolist(). Let us find out how:

```
>>>; from zipfile import ZipFile
>>> import datetime >>>;file="Demo.zip"
>>>; with ZipFile(file,'r') as zip: for information inside zip.infolist():
print(info.filename)
print( 'tModified:t'\ str(datetime.\datetime(*info.date_time)
```

```
print( 'tSystem:tt' \str(info.\create_\system )'
(0=Windows,3=Unix )')
print('tZIP version:t'\ str(info.\create_\version))
print( 'tCompressed:t\' str(info.\compress_\size )' bytes')
print( 'tUncompressed:t' \str(info.\file_\size )' bytes')
```

Demo/1.txt

Modified: 2018-06-15 17:56:32

System: 0(0=Windows,3=Unix)

ZIP version: 20

 Compressed: 0 bytes

Uncompressed: 0 bytes

Demo/2.txt

Modified: 2018-06-15 17:57:18

System: 0(0=Windows,3=Unix)

ZIP version: 20

Compressed: 29 bytes

Uncompressed: 40 bytes

Demo/3.txt

Modified: 2018-06-15 17:56:42

System: 0(0=Windows,3=Unix)

ZIP version: 20

Compressed: 0 bytes

Uncompressed: 0 bytes

THE MOST POPULAR PYTHON PROGRAMMING MISTAKES, AND HOW YOU CAN STAY AWAY FROM THEM

Python is remarkably popular, it's a high-level programming language, largely due to its relative simplicity in comparison to several other notable languages, like C++ and Java. It's particularly great in producing data structures, but it's additionally compatible with just about all platforms: another reason why it's a crowd-pleaser. Having said that, you can still find a selection of typical traps that developers are able to get into when programming in Python, primarily because of wrongly assuming the simplicity of its doesn't include subtlety.

The wrong use of expressions, particularly as default when making purpose arguments Just about the most appealing chances of Python would be that the language enables purpose arguments being specified as suggested, simply by producing a default value because of this performance argument. But simply speaking, it's completely wrong to assume this is going to happen each time a purpose is requested because the worth will continue to have to be prescribed.

This particular mistake happens in those cases in which the default expression which you're wanting to apply is mutable. The problem here's that evaluation was just played out one time when the meaning of the performance took place. This is the main oversight developers are able to make.

```
>>> def foo(bar=None):
...    if bar is None:      # or if not bar:
...       bar = []
...    bar.append("baz")
...    return bar
...
```

```
>>> foo()
["baz"]
>>> foo()
["baz"]
>>> foo()
["baz"]
```

Not using category variables as they ought to be used Class variables are obviously vastly helpful, but their usage to be followed carefully. However, the problem could develop as a class attribute of Python is attributable to a course instead of a characteristic pertaining to the example of a category. It's then crucial that you stay within the comprehension of the method in which the consequent category variables really adhere to a way Resolution Order, due to the problem of several inheritances. To put it briefly, the Python product is going to handle these variables as dictionaries.

Creating a different block but producing the incorrect specifying parameters exception blocks will regularly be needed, but be certain you don't improperly recommend the parameters. When producing several exceptions, the very first exception has to be specified as a tuple, which is a regular sequence information sort.

```
>>> try:
...     l = ["a", "b"]
...     int(l[2])
... except ValueError, IndexError:   # To catch both exceptions, right?
...     pass
...
Traceback (most recent call last):
```

File "<stdin>", line 3, in <module>

IndexError: list index out of range

A failure to grasp the scoping rules for Python

This is a common error occur, because many developers come at Python with a background in another programming language, such as C++, and then there is a failure to appreciate that the scoping rules are in fact a little different. What would be highly recommended is to get a handle on LEGB, which is what Python uses when searching for names. In short, it is:

L – Local

E – Enable

G – Global

B – Built-ins

With an appreciation of this rule, the approach to scoping variables can be differentiated from the approach in other languages, avoiding a crossover.


```
>>> x = 10
>>> def foo():
...    x += 1
...    print x
...
>>> foo()
```


Utilizing expertise of Java to motivate get/set operates If you're coming out of a Java history, obviously, you are going to be acquainted with the very best exercise technique of determining the' getter' and' setter' performs when needing to use the people of a course. But this will provide almost no advantage of Python, for a ream of additional code.

 it is typical being affected by what you're used to, though it will be to the advantage of yours here to keep in mind It is okay in Python to take immediate entry or maybe manipulation of a category member, and you are able to additionally use property decorators to buy the performance you're searching for.

Iterating over a listing, however attempting to alter it at the very same time

Many developers are going to be conscious of this Python unique problem of deletion of something coming from a listing at exactly the same time it's being iterated over. That's not to suggest that mistakes can and can nonetheless be made.

Usually, the solution is usually to simply keep it very simple since the rule of thumb will be that very simple code will be not as likely to suffer from this problem. List comprehensions will also be an excellent way of staying away from this specific pitfall.

```
>>> odd = lambda x : bool(x % 2)
>>> numbers = [n for n in range(10)]
>>> for i in range(len(numbers)):
...    if odd(numbers[i]):
...        del numbers[i]  # BAD: Deleting item from a list while
iterating over it
...
Traceback (most recent call last):
    File "<stdin>", line 2, in <module>
```

IndexError: show index from range

Not understanding the way where variables are bound around closures with Python

The main cause of this common issue is pretty easy to clarify: it's due to the late binding fashion of Python. All of it boils down on the timing of the calling of the internal performance and also the varying values employed in the closures.

Thankfully, the answer is very straightforward too, in it is actually a good deal of a hack: simply produce anonymous features. Almost all you're actually doing is exploiting the default argument.

Just like errors made in numerous other fields of endeavor, like talking a second language, programming problems in Python will primarily develop from reliance in the methods as well as procedures employed inside your experience words - that's the mother tongue of yours is we had been to keep the spoken words metaphor. By appreciating these subtleties in the manner the Python language works, succeeding mistakes could stay away from.

PRECISELY WHY IS PYTHON THE BEST SUITED PROGRAMMING LANGUAGE FOR MACHINE LEARNING?

Machine Learning may be the hottest trend these days. Machine learning patents increased at a 34% pace between 2013 plus 2017 and This is just set to rise down the road. And Python is the main programming language used for a lot of research as well as advancement in Machine Learning. A lot to ensure that Python is the best programming language for Machine Learning according.

Explanations on why Python is Best Suited for Machine Learning?

Python is presently the most used programming language for development and research in Machine Learning. Though you do not need to take the word of mine for it! Based on Google Trends, the curiosity in Python for Machine Learning has spiked to an all-new high along with other ML languages like R, Julia, Scala, Java, etc. lagging far behind.

Now we've determined Python is definitely the most used programming language for Machine Learning, the Why still remains. very let's now comprehend why Python is really so well known and consequently why it's best suited for ML. Several of these reasons for this are provided as follows:

1. Python is not difficult To Use

Nobody likes most difficult things while the ease of utilizing Python is among the primary explanations why it's very popular for Machine Learning. It's easy with an easily readable syntax which causes it to be well-loved by both experienced developers in addition to experimental pupils. The distinctiveness of Python suggests that developers are able to concentrate on just fixing the device Learning issue instead of investing almost all the time of theirs (and energy!) understanding only the specialized nuances of the vocabulary.

Furthermore, Python is additionally supremely effective. It allows for developers to finish more labor using fewer lines of code. The Python code is additionally easily understandable by humans, and that helps make it perfect for making Machine Learning versions. Along with these benefits, what is not to love?!!

2. Python has numerous Libraries & Frameworks

Python has already been very popular and consequently, it's a huge selection of various frameworks and libraries that may be used by developers. These frameworks and libraries are very useful in not wasting time which makes Python a lot more popular (That's an advantageous cycle!!!).

There are lots of Python libraries that are particularly helpful for Artificial Intelligence and Machine Learning. Several of these are provided below:

Keras is an open-source library that is especially focused on experimentation with serious neural networks.

TensorFlow is a totally free software library that is utilized for a lot of machine learning applications including neural networks. (They appear to be rather popular!)

Scikit-learn is a totally free application library for Machine Learning that different classification, regression & clustering algorithms associated with this particular. Additionally, Scikit-learn could be used in conjugation with SciPy and NumPy.

3. Python has Corporate Support and Community

Python has been existing since 1990 and that's ample time to make a supportive community. Due to this particular assistance, Python learners can readily improve the Machine Learning knowledge of theirs, which just results in increasing popularity. And that is not everything! There are lots of resources available on the web to advertise ML in Python, which range from GeeksforGeeks Machine Learning tutorials to YouTube tutorials which are a huge aid for learners.

Additionally, Corporate assistance is a really crucial component of the achievements of Python for ML. Many best businesses, for example, Google, Quora, Netflix, Instagram, Facebook, etc utilize Python for the products theirs. In reality, Google is single-handedly to blame for producing most of the Python libraries for Machine Learning like Keras, TensorFlow, etc.

4. Python is Extensible and portable

This is a crucial reason why Python is very well known in Machine Learning. A lot of cross-language operations can be performed quite easily on Python due to its extensible and portable nature. There are lots of details scientists that like using Graphics Processing Units (GPUs) for teaching the ML models of theirs on the own machines of theirs as well as the lightweight dynamics of Python are effectively designed for this particular.

Additionally, a number of different platforms support Python, for example, Windows, Solaris, Linux, Macintosh, etc. Furthermore, Python may additionally be incorporated with Java,, NET pieces or maybe C/C++ libraries due to the extensible nature of its.

JOB OF PYTHON IN IMAGE APPLICATIONS

Python is a top-level programming language that allows you to work faster and integrate the systems of yours more effectively. ninety % of individuals prefer Python over some other technology due to the simplicity of its, reliability and straightforward interfacing. It's frequently than Lisp, Tcl, Perl, Ruby, C#, Visual Basic, Visual Fox Pro, Java or Scheme. It can easily be quickly interfaced with C/ObjC/Java/Fortran. It runs on almost all major operating systems, for example, Windows, Amiga, Mac, OS/2, Linux/Unix, etc. Day by day we are able to see an immediate growth of Python Development.

Python supports several programming paradigms and modules. Python is supported by the Internet Communications Engine (ICE) as well as numerous other integration solutions. It's packed with rich libraries and lots of add-on packages to tackle certain tasks. Python is a helpful language you are able to discover it effortlessly. Python utilized in numerous businesses, government, nonprofit organizations, Google search engines, YouTube, NASA, the brand new York Stock Exchange, etc. Python is commonly utilized as a scripting language but is additionally utilized in a broad range of non scripting contexts. It offers readable and clear every syntax. You can quickly write programs making use of this language. The Python code runs a lot more than quick enough for many applications. It's utilized in a number of application domains. Python is a superb language for mastering object orientation.

Apps created in Python

Web Applications (Django, Pylons) Games (Eve Online - MMORPG).

3d CAD/CAM.

Picture Applications.

Science as well as Education Applications.

Software Development (Trac for Project Management).

Object Databases (ZODB / Durus).

Network Programming (Bittorent).

Mobile applications.

Audio/Video Applications.

Business Applications.

Console Applications.

Business Applications.

File Formats.

Online Applications.

Python in Image Applications Always pictures have a huge part in achieving the market than the text in the net program area. Simply because a photo may be worth a 1000 words. Usually, some users are able to satisfy the present photos though some users wish to make little changes or creativity to a picture. To be able to fulfill the demands Python of theirs offers various programs. Let us find out how Python utilized in imaging applications

Gnofract 4D is a flexible fractal model plan, enables the user to produce images that are beautiful called fractals. According to mathematical principles, the pc made the pictures automatically are the Julia and Mandelbrot sets and many others. It does not imply you have to do the math for producing the pictures. Rather you are able to use the mouse of yours to develop more images as per the wish of yours. Generally it uses Unix based methods like Freebsd and Linux allowing it to additionally be operated on Mac OS X. It's really convenient to use, really fast, and adaptable with a limitless number of vast amounts and fractal functions of options. It's a commonly used open-source program.

Gogh is a PyGTK based painting plan or maybe a picture editor with support for pressure-sensitive tablets/devices.

ImgSeek is a photo collection supervisor as well as a person with a content-based search. It's several features. If you would like to find a specific item, you just sketch the image or maybe you are able to use another image in the collection of yours. It offers you everything you precisely need.

VPython would be the Python programming language along with a 3d graphics module known as "visual". By making use of it you are able to effortlessly create objects within 3d space as well as animations etc. It allows you to display the items in a window. VPython enables the programmers to focus considerably more on the computational element of the programs of theirs.

MayaVi is a systematic visualization application according to the Visualization Toolkit (VTK), which supports volume visualization of information by feel as well as ray cast mappers. It's simple to use. It may be shipped as a Python module from additional Python packages and could additionally be scripted out of the Python interpreter.

PYTHON PROGRAMMING TIPS

Tip #1: Code Everyday: Consistency is really important when you're learning a brand new language. We recommend committing to coding every single day. It might be difficult, but muscle mind plays a big part in programming. Committing to coding each day will truly help create that muscle memory. Although it might seem daunting in the beginning, think about starting small and coding for twenty-five minutes every day. Then work your way up from there.

Tip #2: Write It Out: As you advance on the journey, you might question when you should start taking notes. Indeed, you need to! In reality, a study shows that taking notes manually is very good for long-term retention. This is going to be particularly good for those working toward becoming a full-time developer, as lots of interviews will involve writing code on a whiteboard.

As soon as you begin to focus on small programs and projects, writing by hand could additionally help you to prepare the code before you transition to the pc. Writing out which classes and functions you are going to need will save you a great deal of time.

Tip #3: Go Interactive!

Regardless of whether you're studying fundamental Python information structures (strings, lists, dictionaries, etc.) for the first time or you're debugging an application, the active Python shell is one of the best learning tools. We put it to use a lot on this site as well!

To utilize the active Python shell (also known as "Python REPL"), first, be sure that Python is installed on your computer. We have a step-by-step tutorial that will help you accomplish that. To activate the synergistic Python layer, just open your terminal and run python or maybe python3 based on your installed version. You will discover much more specific information there.

Now that you know how to start the shell, below are a few examples of how you can use the shell while you're learning:

Learn what operations can be performed on an element by using dir():

>>> my_string = 'I am a string'

>>> dir(my_string)

['__add__', ..., 'upper', 'zfill'] # Truncated for readability

The elements returned from dir() are all of the methods (i.e. actions) that you can apply to the element. For example:

>>> my_string.upper()

>>> 'I AM A STRING'

Notice that we called the upper() method. Can you see what it does? It makes all of the letters in the string uppercase! Learn more about these built-in methods under "Manipulating strings" in this tutorial.

Learn the different types of an element:

>>> type(my_string)

>>> str

Use the built-in help system to get full documentation:

>>> help(str)

Import libraries and play with them:

```
>>> from datetime import datetime
>>> dir(datetime)
['__add__', ..., 'weekday', 'year']  # Truncated for readability
>>> datetime.now()
datetime.datetime(2018, 3, 14, 23, 44, 50, 851904)
```

Run shell commands:

```
>>> import os
>>> os.system('ls')
python_hw1.py python_hw2.py README.txt
```

Tip #4: Take Breaks When you are learning: It is crucial to step away for a while and absorb the concepts. The Pomodoro Technique is famous and can also help: study for 5 minutes, take a short rest, and replicate the process. Taking breaks is essential to having a very effective study session, particularly when you are studying new information.

Breaks are particularly crucial when you are debugging. If you see a bug you can't truly figure out at that point, take a break. Step away from the pc, walk around, or perhaps discuss the bug with your friend.

In programming, your code has to follow the standards of a language. Different eyes make a massive difference.

Tip #5: Become a Bug Bounty Hunter: Speaking of hitting a bug, it is unavoidable once you start writing complex applications. You'll encounter bugs in your code. It's the case with nearly all of us! Don't allow bugs to frustrate you. Instead, embrace these events with pride and think of yourself as a bug bounty hunter.

When debugging, it is important that you have a methodological strategy that will help you discover where everything is breaking down. Move through the code and find out where the problem is so you can fix it.

When you have an idea of where the issues might be, check the subsequent code type inside your software import pdb; pdb.set_trace() and run it. This is the Python debugger and it will help you return to your energetic mode. The debugger might also be operated from the command line with python -m pdb<my_file.py>,</my_file.py>

Enable it being Collaborative When things are going to stick, expedite the learning of yours via cohesiveness. Allow me to talk about various ways to help you get the very best out of working for others.

Tip #6: Surround yourself with other individuals who are also learning: Coding may look like a solitary activity, it is even better when you work together with others. It is very important that you surround yourself with other people who might be learning too when you are learning how to code in Python. This could help you discuss the tricks as well as ideas you learn in the process.

Don't be bothered about not knowing anyone. You are going to find lots of strategies and meet others who are excited about learning Python! Find local events or perhaps meet-ups or maybe subscribe to PythonistaCafe, a peer-to-peer learning class for Python fanatics like you!

Tip #7: Teach: It has been proved that the fastest method of learning something is to teach it. This is exactly how to learn Python. You can teach other Python lovers using the whiteboard, you can publish articles describing newly found principles, record films to describe what you have learned. Each one of these methods will solidify your comprehension of what you have learned.

Tip #8: Pair Program: Pair programming involves two designers running one workstation to complete a task. The two designers transition between getting the "driver" and the "navigator." The "driver" generates the code, although the "navigator" helps to point out the problem and review the code as it is produced.

Pair programming has many advantages. The first is that it provides you with the opportunity to have someone evaluate your code as well as discover exactly how somebody else may imagine a problem. To be subjected to many methods as well as opinions will help your problem-solving skills when you return to your personal coding.

Tip #9: Ask "GOOD" Questions: People generally say that there is no such thing as a bad problem; however, with respect to programming, it is possible to ask a question severely. When you request the help of an individual who has little or no knowledge of the problem you are trying to resolve, it is better to ask questions that are Good using the acronym:

G: Give context on what you are trying to do, clearly describing the problem.

O: Outline the things you have really attempted to resolve the issue.

O: Offer the greatest guess of yours regarding exactly what the problem might be. This will tell the individual who is helping you to find out what you are thinking understand that you have done some thinking as well.

D: Demo what is happening. Include the code, a trace-back error message, as well as a description of the steps you took that resulted in the mistakes. This way, the person helping you will not replicate the problem.

Questions that are Good could save you a good deal of time. Skipping these steps will result in back-and-forth interactions, which could result in conflict. As a beginner, you have to ask questions that are great so that the people supporting you will be happy to help you.

Most, if not all, Python developers you speak with will help you to realize your dream to learn Python. Performing exercises can only help you move quite far; you discover the greatest by creating.

Tip #10: Build Something, Anything For newbies: You will find a lot of small exercises that will certainly help you feel at ease with Python, in addition to creating the muscle memory we spoke about above. When you have a good grasp of the essential information structures (strings, lists, dictionaries, and sets), object-oriented programming, and composting classes, it's time to start creating!

What you build is considerably less important than the strategy you used to build it. The trip to the building is actually what's going to train you the very best. You'll learn a lot by studying Real Python articles along with applications. The bulk of the learning is likely to come from using Python to create something. The problems you're likely to solve will help you greatly.

You will find scores of lists around with techniques for beginner Python tasks. Below are several suggestions to help you get started:

Amount guessing game

Simple calculator app

Dice roll simulator

Bitcoin Price Notification Service

Whenever you feel it's difficult to create Python workout duties to concentrate on, view the video. It states the different ways you can make use of a substantial number of project suggestions any time you feel bored.

Tip #11: Open-Source Help: In the open-source layout, the software package source code can be accessed publicly, and individuals can collaborate. You will find scores of Python libraries, which are open source projects you can practice with. Moreover, a lot of companies publish open-source projects. This means that you're allowed to use the code created and produced by the designers employed in these firms.

Adding to an open-source Python project is a great method of obtaining helpful learning experiences. Imagine if you decide to publish a bug fix request: you post a "pull request" for the fix to be patched into the code.

The project managers will certainly go through what you have done, making comments and suggestions. This will help you learn the best practices for Python programming, in addition to having meaningful conversations with other designers.

www.ingramcontent.com/pod-product-compliance
Lightning Source LLC
Chambersburg PA
CBHW071248050326
40690CB00011B/2303